PokerWoman™

PokerWoman™ ♥♣♦♠

How to Win at **LOVE, LIFE, and BUSINESS**
using the Principles of POKER

Ellen Leikind

Mary Ann Liebert, Inc. publishers

Library of Congress Cataloging-in-Publication Data

Leikind, Ellen.
  PokerWoman : how to win at love, life, and business using the principles of poker /
Ellen Leikind.
      p. cm.
  Includes index.
  ISBN 978-1-934854-22-8
  1. Success. 2. Success in business. 3. Women—Psychology. 4. Poker players—
Psychology. I. Title.
  BF637.S8L436 2010
  650.1—dc22

                                                                      2009042335

Mary Ann Liebert, Inc.
140 Huguenot Street
New Rochelle, NY 10801

Printed in the United States of America.

To POB. The most lovely PrimaDiva there ever was.

Contents

Preface

PokerWoman™ is not a how-to poker book. It is a book about using the principles of poker to enhance your life. Poker is a game about reading people and making informed decisions. It rewards aggression, action, and calculated risk taking. Poker requires discipline, good decision-making, and the ability to adjust to life's twists and turns. It is an unpredictable game so you need to figure out what elements you can control to get the edge. Reading other people, not giving off any of your own nonverbal cues ("tells" in poker), managing your money, understanding the odds, and choosing the right game and opponents are all skills that can help you get the edge.

I am not a professional poker player, although I like the game very much. I am a professional business woman with an MBA in marketing. After 15 years working in escalating marketing positions for Fortune 500 companies, I decided to take a one year hiatus from the corporate grind and started playing Texas Hold 'Em poker on a consistent basis. The more I played, the more I saw the similarities between the game and the larger "game" of business and personal achievement. I then founded POKERprimaDIVAS®, a company that provides corporations and individuals programs and entertainment by teaching women how to play poker, and how to use the principles acquired at the poker table to enhance their business skills.

For those who have never played a game of Texas Hold 'Em, here is a quick summary of the game: Each person is dealt two "hole" cards (face down cards), which are theirs exclusively. Up to five more community cards will come out—the "flop" (the first three cards in unison), the "turn" (the fourth card, otherwise known as "fourth street"), and the fifth card ("fifth street"), also known as "the river." These five community cards belong to everyone still in the hand. The job of the player is to make the best five-card hand using a combination of hole cards and community cards. The beginner reading this book may pick up a few tips about the game, but everyone will pick up the larger lessons of poker that enhance one's chance of winning in life, relationships, and business. Enjoy!

ELLEN LEIKIND

Acknowledgments

I could not have finished this book without the guidance, moral support, and friendship of Blanche Brann who knew when I needed a push to keep going and was always ready to lend a hand when I was at my wits end. Thanks to Karen Kapowitz for her ongoing support of all things POKERprimaDIVAS® and for introducing me to Blanche.

To the powers that be that allowed me to meet Mary Ann Liebert on a Saturday afternoon at Harvard, discussing the value of Poker Theory in the law school. Mary Ann, I am grateful for your friendship and collaboration in putting together *PokerWoman* and look forward to seeing where the journey takes us.

To all the people at Mary Ann Liebert Publishing for their kindness, time, support, and patience during this project: Vicki Cohn, Larry Bernstein, Georgia Prince, Julia Chapman, Esther Bicovny, Marianne Russell, Cathia Falvey, Bill Schappert, and Catherine Censor who knew how to put things into words when I couldn't. I am also grateful to Melody Negron who handled many of the production details.

I thank my mother, Simone Leikind, for teaching me the game even though I was probably a bit young to learn it, and for her insight, advice, and support in writing this book. I thank my father, Seymour Leikind, for his marketing expertise, and for helping me with creative issues and putting all the pieces together—and, of course, I am grateful for his outstanding PowerPoints.

Thanks to the Ideavillage meditation crew, that I am ever so happy to get up at the crack of dawn to spend mornings with: Andy Khubani, Ron Boger, Maryann Hrebeniuk, Robin Bonnema, Jo Anne Grassa, Alex Gilroy, Lana Rascionato, and Daniella Rascionato. This has been a great gift and everyday it gets better. Thank you, Laura Nash for helping my mind and spirit thrive, and opening up new pathways to follow. To all my friends at Ideavillage, I am lucky to have the opportunity to spend time with people who I like so much: Brenda, Lana, George, Lori-Ann, David, Kyle, John, Alfredo, Mark, Marc, Michelle, Janine, Theresa, Tonya, Mahesh, Tim, Rishad, Wendy, Nancy, Tracy, Karen, Jim, Cathy, Bena, and Debbie.

My heartfelt thanks to Lori Klausner for her many great stories, ideas, spirit, remarkable positive energy, and willingness to always lend an ear and see the bright side.

My appreciation to Jamie Falk, Jill Lambert, and Andrew Batwin for their honest, compelling stories and experiences, and to my Wednesday night poker crew, Jamie, Bob, Jon, Pat, Erica, SJ, Nadge, Flip, Richard, Ken, James, Aner, Lori, and Ron for telling me all their stories and listening to mine. And thanks to Avia and Abby for their home cooking and hospitality.

Thanks to Bill Hyman for letting me take over his computer so I could make my deadline.

I am grateful to Anand Dhirmalani for his plentiful wisdom and support in poker and in life; to Faith Gingold, Donna Landau, Stan Choy, and Monica Kornblum for their never ending moral support; and to Zoe Rice for making me sound better even if she sometimes only had a short time in which to do it.

I do not know what I would do without Joseph Meagher, Makiko Ono, and Jacob to keep my hair, body, and mind in shape.

Thank you, Barrie Rosen and Barry Silberzweig for giving me a place to go on Madison Avenue, and David Jacobson and Wendy Lasker for giving me a home and a forum for POKERprimaDIVAS®.

I don't know if I would have ever learned to love the game if it were not for Karen Janowsky and her Monday night hospitality and our jaunts to the Borgata in Atlantic City. KJ, thanks for being my first poker partner in crime.

I am so happy that my many POKERprimaDIVAS®, including Millie, Deni, Laurel, Linda, Karen, Mara, Jennifer, Adrienne, Staci, Jon, Deborah, Joy, Melissa, Harriet, Judy, and Karen, found each other and that I found them.

Kendall Ridgeway, and Joe Parnett, and Ellen Simpson, thank you for knowing I can always count on you.

To my oldest and dearest, Lindsey Cashman, Barrie Rosen, Lauren Vieland, Sue Townsend, Robert Mongioi, Margie Dwoskin, John Fallon, and Bob Lee who remain in my heart throughout too many years to mention.

Thanks to Audra Guglielmetti, Angelo Santisi, Adrienne Yee, Clarissa Ritter, Cindy Olinger, Elizabeth Perthbery, Gail Knox, Joyce Newman, Kathryn Nielson, Karen Dow, Kathi Kuhne-Giron, Kristin Mineo, Lisa Zaslow, Mara Zuckerman, Paula Szturma, Peter Mineo, Jordan Pine, Stacey Lewis, Steve Rivkin, Steve Fishman, Susan Sommers, and Thomas Novella for all their advice and supporting all that I do.

Many thanks to Kathy Liebert for her inspiring words and for moving women closer to the forefront of poker.

Thank you, Kay Sullivan for taking the best care of and being a second mother to my favorite princess who knew that you can get away with doing it your own way. We miss her very much.

To FS, who inspires me even if he doesn't always know it.

To Daisy, Spencer, Fudgie, Muffins, Timmy and Bailey, Charlie, Freddie and Madison, Kitty, Chloe, Chevalier and Petite Dejeuner, Betty, Rilo, Farinelli Doougie, and Ava, Ruby, Sammy, Sophie, Fluffy, Rusty, Dolly and Ellie. You make the world go round.

I hope all the readers will find something in here which will help you make your life fuller, your soul deeper, dull your fears, and get your heart pumping with excitement again. Find what you are looking for, ask for what you want, and remember, you never know . . .

And therein it lies . . .

ELLEN LEIKIND

PokerWoman™

Foreword by
Kathy Liebert

Kathy Liebert is presently ranked top woman poker tournament player in the world, with cash earnings over $5,577,000. She also has a gold bracelet won in the 2004 World Series of Poker $1500 shootout.

She is best known as the first woman to win a million dollar prize pool on the Party Poker Millions inaugural cruise, however her success in No Limit tournaments is even more impressive with numerous wins and final tables at the World Series of Poker and World Poker Tour.

I'm a gambler. That's how I make my living, and it is how I made history. It all started when I took my first big gamble and left my job as a business analyst at Dun & Bradstreet without knowing what I was going to do next. Dissatisfied with my job, I listened to my mom, who told me, "Do what you love and the money will follow." That's fine advice—provided you know what you love. I didn't, so I traveled to Colorado to go skiing. I thought it would be a fun place to live and a lot less expensive than New York.

While I was there, I started playing low-limit poker for fun, ultimately getting a job as a "prop," getting paid to play $5-limit poker. Mostly, I did it for my own amusement, but I wondered if I could actually make enough at it to pay the bills. It didn't happen quite that way. Some days, not only did I not *make* money, but I actually *lost* more than my pay. Still, as I didn't have a passion for anything else, I decided to work on my game by discussing poker with successful, more experienced players. Little did I know that taking a chance on something I loved would lead me to a very lucrative poker career!

The first couple of years, I played low-limit poker in the casinos and played some home games that regularly took place in Denver. There weren't many women playing poker for a living, and men generally looked at a woman as dead money and the weakest player at the table. I saw their skepticism as just another challenge to overcome and I was up for it. In 1994, a few friends from Colorado were going to Las Vegas to play a poker tournament, and invited me to join them. I thought it would be a good test to see if I had the skills to win in Vegas. I bought a book on poker tournament strategy and studied it.

The first tournament I played, a $120 buy-in with more than 400 entrants, I found myself heads-up and made a deal to chop the money (split the pot). A few days later, I found myself heads-up in another tournament and chopped it again. After one week in Vegas, I had won more than $35,000, and began to think I might be able to make my living playing poker. I was focused and money came easily in those first few months of playing tournaments as I followed my initial success with many more wins and final tables. Little did I know what was to come.

In 1995, the wins did not come as easily. The tournament trail was a tough way to make an "easy" living. I had to have a top spot just to cover expenses. However, I did enjoy the challenge, and I thrived on the competition. I had many ups and downs, but continued to make some final tables and wins. I wasn't making a fortune, but I was enjoying the challenge of the game.

In 2002, the Internet poker boom had begun, and Party Poker was holding a tournament with a $1 million guarantee for first place. I won that tournament—which included Phil Hellmuth and Chris Ferguson at the final table—to become the first woman to win a tournament with a $ 1 million prize. A huge accomplishment? Yes. A welcome enhancement of my bankroll? Absolutely. Then, in 2004, I won a Limit Hold 'Em event at the World Series of Poker for my first gold bracelet. I had become the world's leading woman tournament winner.

Nothing can top the feeling of winning tournaments, but the rewards of poker playing, for me, have not been entirely monetary.

Poker has given me an invaluable set of skills. I have learned that poker is not only about playing the cards, but is also about playing the people. I began labeling and categorizing players in order to use their weaknesses and strengths to my advantage. My woman's intuition gave me a slight edge that I soon recognized would puzzle and, yes, even confuse some players. Women are more in tune with their feelings and emotions than men. It's an inherent trait we should utilize in all facets of our lives, but never more so than at the poker table. Tapping into your natural talent and senses are strong allies in developing strategies in the game. But I also learned to push myself to be more aggressive. A passive style is more common among women players, but checking and calling is not great poker strategy. Overly aggressive males will often try to bluff you if you show weakness, and you do need to confront them and be willing to raise sometimes, even when you don't hold a good hand.

Along with winning at poker, managing your money is an important skill to survive in the poker world. Many successful players play above their bankroll. They gamble big and wind up going broke. I told people that I was never going to go broke, a pledge always greeted with derision.

That is where my interest in investing paid off and kept me from suffering the same fate as many other skilled players. Rather than play high or gamble when I had my tournament wins, I would invest the money. Once you have success, whether in poker or your career, if you do not wisely manage your money, it can all vanish as quickly as it arrived. I think the skills necessary to be a winning poker player are similar to the skills necessary to be a winning stock market investor. You need to take some calculated risks, and you also need a bit of luck. Investing in risky stocks or hands can yield big rewards as well as big losses.

I have one more challenge still out there—to be recognized as one of the very best poker players *without the gender label*. But in the meantime, I cherish my many wins, both professional and personal.

Poker has taught me patience, control of my emotions, the ability to act decisively, and the skills to manage both people and finances. This book will present many examples, methods, and scenarios that will guide you to your own success at poker, your career, or in your personal life. Find your strengths and capitalize on them and recognize your weaknesses and learn from them. This book will furnish you with the tools to do both. Whatever you want out of life, no matter what your goals might be, always remember that *preparation* meets *opportunity*. So set the bar high and reach for that "gold" bracelet!

Introduction

If you think you are not a poker player, think again. In many ways, you've been playing poker your whole life, even if you've never shuffled a deck of cards. Poker is about evaluating and making the best of the hand you are dealt, reading other people, knowing when to be assertive, managing your money, and calculating risk—or as they say at the poker table, knowing when to go all-in and knowing when to get out. The same traits that have made you successful in life, business, and relationships are also what constitute a good poker player. Women already have a natural propensity to many of the qualities that make great poker players: keen powers of observation, uncanny intuition, multitasking dexterity, and the willingness to assume risk. Whether you're a take-charge woman in a male-dominated profession or a more retiring sort who avoids confrontation at all costs, poker can help you tap into your innate strengths and intelligence. As you will soon learn, knowing how to play a good game of poker can also enhance the skills that can put your career and personal ambitions within your grasp. There's a PokerWoman™ inside of you, and she's waiting to be unleashed!

For many of us, the toughest challenge is taking that first step: taking your seat at the table. Look around a poker room at a casino anywhere in the world and you'll notice that there's a tremendous similarity between those seated and the list of the top 500 executives in corporate America. Both are filled with testosterone and typically, very few women. Unfortunately, that's the reality of the upper echelons of the business world, too. Don't let this deter you.

You will learn that poker sharpens not only strategic thinking, but also psyche. It helps build confidence, encourages assertiveness and risk taking, and teaches how to read nonverbal cues. In many ways, it's a game about playing people, not cards. When I went back to work, in a more entrepreneurial capacity, I noticed that many of the skills I had acquired at the poker table translated to other areas of my personal and professional life. I also noticed that there were not many women playing the game, which was a detriment to them professionally. Not only is the game great for honing business skills, but it has become a major networking tool.

Poker has become the "new golf." It's a networking sport where alliances and friendships are forged, contacts are made, and deals get done. Several years ago, I noticed that an increasing number of corporate events (sales meetings, training sessions, etc.) culminated in a game of poker. The kingpins and rainmakers were having an awfully good time getting to know each other in a more relaxed circumstance. So it dawned on me that if you wanted to network and enhance your situation, poker was the key to entry. Women were going to have to learn to play poker if they wanted to succeed on a professional level.

If you think about it, there's no reason why poker shouldn't be an equal opportunity game. To play a great game of poker, you don't need to be particularly physically fit. You don't need to be particularly adept at sports. What you do need you already have in abundance, and what you lack, you're about to learn. In poker, as in life, if you're not playing, you can't win.

The woman who dares to take a seat at the table, despite prevailing social norms, is usually strong, focused, knows what she wants, assertive when she needs to be, and very aware of her surroundings. She's in tune with others' strengths and weaknesses, as well as her own. She listens to her own good instincts. And she knows the importance of being patient. Those are the things that make someone a winning poker player, and a PokerWoman™.

Over time, the real winners at this game, and the real winners in business and other aspects of life, are not the bullies or the reckless risk-takers—they're those who maintain a missile-like focus on their goals. They're women like Madeleine Albright, Hillary Rodham Clinton, and Madonna, who aren't just talented people who "caught a lucky break." They are persistent, enduring, and above all, adaptable, trying their hand at different careers or life experiences and seizing opportunities. They may stumble (anyone remember Madonna in *Shanghai Surprise?*) But they win more often than they lose. I don't know whether they play cards, but I am certain they're all poker women.

Above all, poker is an equal opportunity springboard. We all are dealt two unique cards (the hole cards) and we all play with the same set of community cards. We need to use our inimitable talents and leverage them to our advantage to achieve our goals. You don't have to be the most experienced, the best educated, or the most beautiful to succeed. Look at one of America's favorites, Oprah Winfrey. What were the chances that an African-American woman who wasn't a size six, born wealthy, or Ivy-League educated would become one of the most influential women in the country, not to mention an international media mogul? So, don't think for a second that you can't be the chip leader. But in order to win, you've got to be in the game.

1
The Four Types of Players

In a poker game, getting to know your competition can mean the difference between losing and winning. How they play, why they play, and when they make certain moves are all things you need to be looking at. As your powers of observation continue to improve, you'll soon know with certainty whether your opponent is meek or bold, focused or spacey, a leader or a follower, so you can adjust your play accordingly. The basic objective in poker is to win as much money as you can, while risking as little as possible. The interesting thing about poker is that you don't necessarily need the best hand to win. You just need to make sure that other people *think* that you have the best hand. As Anthony Holden, author of *Big Deal*, says, "The good news is that in every deck of fifty-two cards there are 2,598,960 possible hands. The bad news is that you are only going to be dealt one of them."

Betting is really the crux of the game, because when you bet (put money in the pot), or when you raise somebody else's bet, you are giving the other people at the table information. You are telling them you have something good, or at least you want them to think you have something good. Whether you are telling the truth is irrelevant in poker. You have to convince your opponents that you have the best hand and they are going to try to do the same. So how do you figure out who really has the goods and who is bluffing? You need to establish the identities of the frequent bettors, then determine how much they bet, when they bet, and when they fold.

When you're at the table, you'll notice there are many different types of poker players. And as you begin to play more often, you'll see that the way people play their poker game reflects their personality at work, in relationships, and in social situations.

A poker player's playing style or personality is a combination of aggressiveness, passiveness, tightness, and looseness.

Here are the four different types of poker personalities:
- ♥ Passive/Loose
- ♦ Passive/Tight
- ♠ Aggressive/Loose
- ♣ Aggressive/Tight

(Missile) Oprah Condoleezza Rice Suze Orman Meg Whitman	**(Bully)** Ann Coulter Rosanne Barr Rush Limbaugh	↑ **Aggressive**
(Casper the Friendly Ghost) Mary Poppins Jane Doe	**Sidekick** (Calling Station) Ed McMahon Ethel Mertz	**Passive** ↓
◄‖‖‖ **Tight**	**Loose** ‖‖‖►	

Passive/Loose = Higher Risk, Low Reward

Typically, about half of the beginning poker players we see playing are passive/loose players otherwise known as "calling stations." A calling station is somebody who just wants to be in the game, but never takes the initiative. If you put in a bet, they'll match your bet. They're not going to raise you or challenge you. They are not going to make a bet on their own. They are followers, not leaders. It is very hard, when you play with a calling station, to bluff them because they tend to want to stay in the hand. A typical calling station is like a sidekick—Ed McMahon to Johnny Carson or Ethel to Lucy. He or she doesn't want to take the risks

Away from the Table
Romance with a Calling Station

Being in a romantic relationship with a calling station can be a very frustrating experience, especially for a successful woman. It may be great at the beginning because you are with someone who seems very agreeable, but over time it gets difficult to be in a long-term relationship with a calling station because the other party never initiates any decisions.

A friend of mine, Susan, dated a man for six months and was in heaven because this guy did everything she asked. They ate wherever she suggested, they took a great trip to Budapest that she planned, and they saw whatever movie or concert she picked. He was only too happy to do what she asked. She thought he was just a great, agreeable guy.

But after a while, she got very tired of making all the decisions. She felt like the entire weight of the relationship was on her back. So she decided to let him demonstrate that he could, in fact, take the reins occasionally, and asked him to plan a weekend away. He couldn't. That was just not part of his personality. Susan noticed the similarity between her boyfriend and her poker buddy, Paula. Paula never made the first move but would call every bet. Susan saw how this game would play out. She had to be with someone more aggressive.

In a relationship, sometimes the woman is the calling station. She may not be overwhelmingly happy, but she tolerates her situation. There are a lot of women who stay in unsatisfying relationships because they fear being alone. They would rather be unhappy than risk "losing" their current boyfriend. Of course, women who pursue this "safe" strategy fail to realize that it's often anything but! There are hidden costs to maintaining the status quo. Often, it makes sense to put just a little more on the line—in order to get what you really want.

associated with game-changing moves (like raising or initiating a bet); they just want to keep playing. Their strategy might keep them around for a while but they're never really the ones who make it big.

Passive/Tight = Low Risk, Low Reward

This is the person who is fearful of losing money. They will never put in a bet. If you bet them, they will fold their hand. You can easily bluff this person, because they are afraid. You can put in a bet with any hand, and they are going to fold UNLESS they have something very good. And if they do call you, you know they have a hand. These are not "personalities" so much as warm bodies. They are very easy to read. This is the kind of person you want at your poker table. This is the kind of person you want to do a negotiation with—no surprises, good or bad. This is probably not the kind of person you want to be in a relationship with, unless you like the idea of life with a placeholder.

Aggressive/Loose = High Risk, High Reward

If you watch professional poker, the aggressive, loose player is really a bully. (I think Gus Hansen is probably the best example of this type of player.) This person is betting, raising, calling, doing everything to try to intimidate and confuse. They really don't care what kind of cards they have. Obviously, if they have good cards, so much the better, but they're going to play the same kind of game regardless. They are comfortable throwing their weight around, they are not afraid to lose, and they are bold to the point of recklessness. The bully is a skydiver, a racecar enthusiast. He (and it is often a *he*) would bet on the number of days it was going to rain in a month. They crave action. And don't be fooled by the charming bully. He knows how to charm you to get what he wants. He reels you in and then makes his move.

Let's say you're sitting at a poker table, and you know the person three seats to your left raises you every single time you're in the hand. No matter what, they raise you. Well, guess what? That's the kind of person that you can only play good cards against. You're not really going to bluff that person, because they want action.

The same thing would be true if you were in a business situation with somebody who was always trying to get a better deal. No matter what you say, they claim to have a more attractive option at the ready. You have to know that they're going to bargain aggressively, so when you go to negotiate, you leave a lot of room to maneuver.

If you find yourself playing against a bully, you're not going to bluff him. However, if you are getting very good cards, you want to bet in to a bully, because he is not going away. Use his "strength" against him; if he keeps raising you, you're just going to make more money.

If you are dating this type of player, you'd better like the ups and downs. He may make a fun date on occasion, but in the long term he is just too exhausting and indeed, reckless, for an enduring relationship.

Aggressive/Tight = Low Risk, High Reward

This is the ultimate poker player, the missile. This is the person who is not afraid to lose, but is not reckless. They know the right time to go in. They know the right time to get out. When they have a good hand, they enter it very, very aggressively and passionately. Unlike the bully, when they think they're beat, they know when to walk away. If you're playing against a missile, you better be very careful.

If you find yourself dating a missile, you'll quickly note how focused he can be and he'll zero in on you. He'll also figure out pretty quickly if it's the relationship he's been looking for. Missile types know if they want a date, a wife, a friend, or a one-night stand. If you don't match what he's looking for, he'll quickly be on his way. The upside to dating missile-type men is that they rarely jerk you around. If it's a match, okay, but if not, he won't dither and there's nothing you can say or do that's going to change his mind.

Most of the players you will encounter—and many of the people you meet in your daily life—will fall into one of these four types. When you're at the poker table, it's very important to pay attention to the behavior of your competitors. You want to know if you've got a bully or a calling station. It's really not that different from what we do when we start dating someone. And we do it in business all the time. One of the greatest skills that poker teaches is the power of observation, but it does so in a way that is uniquely empirical. In "real life," you make some observations about someone's character and wait until events confirm your suspicions—or fail to. You might wait months or even years before you learn whether you were right. That's not the case in poker, in which confirmation may be as close as your opponent's next move. You can essentially cram a lifetime of experience judging character into just a few hands of poker.

Being able to get a good read on someone can be invaluable. You learn to understand behavior. Don't you love a game where one of the key components to successful play is people-watching?

Playing Your Hand

♣ Know what kind of person you're dealing with.

♣ Play on your terms with a Passive/Loose person, but if you're looking for a true partner, this isn't the type for you.

♣ Act aggressively with a Passive/Tight person, and you'll get what you want.

♣ Hold your ground against an Aggressive/Loose player at the right moment, and you can win a lot, but do not try to bluff them.

♣ You can't necessarily get what you want from the Aggressive/Tight person, but if you do, it will be the best situation for both of you.

Quiz: Which Type of Player Are You?

1. Take charge personality. Circle the letter that best describes you:

    A. I always take charge

    B. I like to take charge when I know something really well

    C. I often like to see what people do before I act

    D. I usually like to see what people do before I act

2. My motto is:

    A. Act now, ask questions later

    B. Get the facts and get ready to go

    C. Wait and see

    D. Better safe than sorry

3. Which would you rather have?

    A. $1 million today

    B. $3 million in 2 years

    C. $5 million in 5 years

    D. $10 million in 10 years

4. When in a group meeting:

    A. You speak more than anyone else in the room

    B. You make a few very relevant points

    C. You chime in and expand on what others have said

    D. You keep quiet and take good notes

5. Your clothing style could best be described as:

    A. Statement-making; I like to be noticed!

    B. Stylish or classic with a twist

    C. Tastefully conservative

    D. I don't like to draw attention to myself

6. When you walk into a room you:

    A. Introduce yourself to everyone you see

    B. Scope out the room for people who you want to meet

C. Talk to whomever talks to you first
D. Stand in the corner and have a drink

7. How would your co-workers describe you?

A. Aggressive
B. Focused
C. Easy Going
D. Quiet

8. Which do you think describes you best?

A. Up for anything
B. Strong and silent
C. Go with the flow
D. Safety first

9. If you won $500 in a lottery which would you most likely do?

A. Spend it then and there on a great night out with friends
B. Spend it on something you have wanted for a while
C. Hold on to it for a while until you see something you want to buy
D. Save it

10. The president of a company you would love to work for walks into a café you are dining at.

A. You walk right up to them and give them your card
B. You walk by them on the way out, tell them how much you admire them and send a follow-up note the next day
C. You smile and hope to catch their eye
D. Nothing, you don't want to disturb them

11. Your romantic relationships are best described as:

A. You have to be the one in charge
B. You share decisions
C. Your partner makes most of the decisions
D. Your partner makes all the decisions

12. How do you handle rejection?

- A. I'm too tough to take it personally
- B. I cry but quickly look for the upside and try to move on
- C. I spend a lot of time trying to figure out what is wrong with me
- D. I feel devastated and stop trying

13. Which describes your reaction when your boyfriend/partner breaks up with you?

- A. Oh well, there are plenty more where he came from!
- B. Sad but the next one will give me more of what I need
- C. I must to have done something to deserve it
- D. I'm convinced I'll never meet anyone again

14. A relative you are not crazy about asks you to be her bridesmaid. You:

- A. Quickly decline, no excuses necessary
- B. Decline with a brief excuse and send a nice note and gift
- C. Say yes, you would be delighted, and just suffer through it
- D. Say yes but dread your decision until the day of the event

15. If you are passed over for a well-deserved promotion, you'd:

- A. Quit on the spot without having another job
- B. Start job-hunting, call all your contacts
- C. Wait another six months to see what happens
- D. Tell yourself you were really not the best person for the job

16. You think:

- A. Very little; you tend to just jump
- B. Very fast on your feet
- C. With great deliberation
- D. Very, very carefully. You tend to over-think

17. Which would you rather do if you had the time and money?

- A. Skydive or fly an airplane
- B. Play a sport you love with a professional player

    C. Have lunch with someone you admire

    D. Watch someone you admire give a speech in person

18. A friend asks you to give a last minute toast at a wedding. You:

    A. Say yes and wing it

    B. Say yes and quickly prepare something clever

    C. Say yes, but only if a friend can do it with you

    D. Decline, you do not like speaking in public

19. You like games that have a high level of:

    A. Competition

    B. Skill and strategy

    C. Team playing

    D. Thinking

20. Which of these compliments which you most like to get?

    A. She is not afraid of anything

    B. She really knows how to take charge of a situation

    C. She is really a good team player

    D. She never ruffles anyone's feathers

Scoring:

Mostly A's: You're an Aggressive/Loose player and a bit of a loose cannon. You crave action. You can win big in poker but you're also capable of crashing at the table. Both in business and in personal relationships, you may need to step back a bit, look before you leap, and focus more attention on specific issues that may best enable you to achieve your goals. You're willing to take chances in life, which is great, but make sure you are using your chips wisely and not being reckless with them. The instant big "all-in" win is a great rush but sometimes a little patience has a bigger payout.

Mostly B's: You're an Aggressive/Tight player. You're focused and purposeful. In short, you have what it takes to become a great poker player. You're very effective in business and you know what you want. Your calculated thinking and actions work well in business but your personal life requires a little more spontaneity. Make sure you don't lose touch with your emotional side, especially when it comes to romantic relationships. Sometimes you have to call a questionable bet to spice things up a little.

Mostly C's: You're a Passive/Loose player, otherwise known as "The calling station." You're along for the ride but never the leader. While you may not lose a lot in poker, you're unlikely to be a big winner. In business, you aren't living up to your potential and need to take the initiative more often, stepping out into the forefront rather than staying behind the scenes. In personal relationships, you cede the decision-making, even when it concerns how a relationship will develop. You are reluctant to set deadlines or make any demands. Practice taking a leadership role sometimes. Lead a project at work or be the one who puts together the evening plans for all your friends or family. Try to identify what you want rather than have someone else do it for you. Learn to be the bettor rather than the caller.

Mostly D's: You're a Passive/Tight player who is most comfortable standing on the sidelines watching everyone else. Unless you get in the game, you will never be a good poker player. You are afraid to loose your chips. Push past your fears, recognize your value, and define your wants and needs. Take the chance on yourself, and give yourself the tools you need to improve your confidence. Travel to a new place, take a course in something that interests you, or become an expert in an area you enjoy. If need be, take a public speaking course like those offered by Dale Carnegie. It can be life changing. If you are unhappy with your looks, hire a personal shopper or stylist or have a friend take you shopping. If you feel you cannot grow within your current environment, think about moving elsewhere. In relationships, make sure people know what you need. There is no point in hanging on to all your chips if you are not having fun playing the game.

2

Getting Your Seat at the Table: Breaking into the Boys' Club

Most businesses are still clubhouses for the boys. Regardless of the profession or how well you may get along with the men in your industry, there is a distinction between the way men and women do business. One woman we spoke to works for an organization heavily populated by men at the more senior levels. As a senior executive, she spends a lot of time with them, unlike the other women in the office, who tend to have the more administrative jobs. While she has no doubt that the men within her group respect her, she also knows that there are times that she is excluded from either a lunch or social outing because she is not "one of the boys." Typically, she'll joke about it, just so that they know that she is aware. And they are aware, but the bottom line is that there is still a boys' club to which she has been denied admission.

The dilemma is plain: How do you get access? Denying a woman access to a board meeting on the basis of her gender might be ridiculous—not to mention legally actionable—but a social occasion is another matter altogether. Whether it's a round of golf, a night at a club, or a game of poker, there are social spaces where women are either totally excluded or made to feel unwelcome. Your presence is cramping their style! You're making it impossible for them to do whatever is the male equivalent of "letting their hair down."

Poker is probably one of the last legitimized boys' clubs. If you walk into the poker room, you'll find that it is 85 percent to 90 percent male dominated. While there are a lot of poker players who work well with women and play well with them, there are also those who aren't used to having them in the room and resent their presence.

Well, that's their problem. You have every right to be in that room. Don't hold your breath waiting to be invited. Ask to be included and be persistent. Even if you get a reluctant invitation to be the token female, take it. Now, that doesn't mean they're going to put you at ease when you first get there. You're going to have to make yourself comfortable. There are some women who are absolutely fearless and have no problem walking into a situation where they're not welcome. But for the rest of us, here are a few tips:

First, walk in with confidence. You must seem fearless, whether or not you actually are. It can be very unnerving to walk into a poker room with 500 men and twenty-five women. Perhaps it's even worse when you're the only woman in a group of ten. The first time you walk into that situation, it's extraordinarily intimidating, but you can do it. It may not feel comfortable at first, but it will get better each time. It's just like your first dance, your first job interview, your first business meeting, or your first public speaking engagement. Even if you're a nervous wreck, put on a brave face. It's okay to fake your confidence. One day—and it won't be long—you won't have to.

The other technique that's helpful is to just watch and listen for a while. Don't walk in and try to make your mark instantly. Feel out the table. See what the different personalities are. Who is potentially your ally? Who do you think is going to be your biggest problem? After you've analyzed the room, you can find your comfort zone. This is an example of how "acting last" can be a good strategic play. Don't throw that advantage away by sitting down at the table, concentrating solely on the cards, and getting into the action too fast; you'll miss an opportunity to understand the players. It's very important to understand who's aggressive, who's passive, who wants to be your friend, and who's already against you.

Watching and learning is a key component, just as it would be in a business situation. Did you ever work with someone who, after being on the job for only a day, walks into a meeting and starts talking about her own agenda without having any idea of the players or protocol? Or a person who is new to a parents' organization who starts spouting off ideas before knowing the goals of the group? It's fine to be assertive, but if you look before you leap you will be more effective.

While you observe, keep in mind that you're not the only one in the room who is likely to feel uncomfortable. It can be unsettling for men to have you on their turf. It's very interesting to see the responses this trespass can provoke. And at the poker table, when confronted with a female opponent, men will typically revert to one of three iconic characters.

One is going to be a bully. You're a female, you shouldn't be there, he's angry that you're there, and he's going to make every effort to try to put you in your place. He may attempt to intimidate you by playing very aggressively against you, by betting back very hard at you, trying to make you fold every hand, and making you fearful. He'll persist in these tactics until either you push him back or you start taking his money. But the good news about the bully is if, in fact, you're getting very good cards at the table, you're going to make a lot of money. That's because he's not going to want to lose to a woman. He is not going to want to fold to you, so as you're betting, he's either raising you or he's betting back, and you stand to win a good amount of cash. Just remember that when playing against a bully, you cannot bluff. He's always coming back at you.

Away from the Table
Working with a Bully

I'm sure you have worked with a guy like this. If he is your superior, he will speak disrespectfully to you in a room full of people, or he may yell at you publicly. Perhaps he knocks down any new idea you bring him and then, two months later, brings up the same idea and pretends it is his own. If he is a subordinate, he may decide to go above your head to your boss and keep you out of the loop. He will attempt to ignore you as he can't stand taking direction from a woman. One of my students, Susan, had a boss who was the worst kind of bully. He would compliment her work when they were in a one-on-one meeting. His praise would motivate her to work even harder. But when they were in their large weekly divisional meeting, he would interrupt her when she spoke or talk over her. He was threatened by her intelligence in front of this large group and used his position to intimidate her. And beware: Men are not the only bullies in the workplace. Women can be just as bad. So do what you do to the bully at the poker table and push back. Stick up for yourself. Call their bets and let them know you have no fear.

The second type of man at the table is the one who sees you as his mother or sister, the Madonna complex. He is going to be very respectful toward you. He may just check or will call all of your bets but he's not going to raise you. He's going to get out of your way when you're raising. He doesn't really want much to do with you, but he's polite and pleasant. He will tolerate your presence, recognizing that you have the right to be there. In life, this is your typical "nice guy."

And then, of course, there's the guy who is looking for a date, Mr. Romeo. I don't think I'm saying anything shocking or new here, but whether it's on a supermarket checkout line, a flight to Chicago, or even at a funeral, there are guys for whom any interaction with a woman is an opportunity to score. Speaking from a purely tactical standpoint (we'll leave ethics to another book), women can use this to their advantage. This is the kind of guy who will fold when he should be raising you. He may flirt openly with you. He may tell you not to call his raises, because he has a good hand. For Mr. Romeo, now that you're at the table, it's ceased to be a game of poker. As far as he's concerned, the two of you are on a date and the poker game is background noise. If maintaining that fiction means losing an extra $50 or $100 to you or not making some money off of somebody else, he's going to do it. The way he sees it, it's a form of passive dating rather than taking you out for dinner or a drink. He doesn't mind losing a couple of bucks to you at the table.

Whether you're sitting down with men for a game of poker or giving a sales presentation, recognize what kind of men are at the table and act accordingly. There are men whom you'll work with that want to date you. There are those who will respect you, although they may or may not want you there. And then there are those who are just going to antagonize you, and they're going to be very competitive with you simply because you're a female.

Away from the Table
Playing with Fire: Trading on Attraction

Lisa and Diane, two attractive 35-plus women, were playing in Atlantic City one night. Lisa convinced Diane to go to the 2/5 no-limit Texas Hold 'Em table and sit with eight men, each with chip stacks upward of $2,000, because Lisa had played with one of the guys before and found him very attractive. The girls each had about $200 in chips.

At first they were nervous about getting involved in a hand, but after about ten minutes, the guys started joking and flirting with them. Everyone was ordering them drinks and having fun. Then Lisa noticed that the most aggressive player at the table who was raising everyone would just call when she bet and never raised her. In fact, there were several instances when these guys could have taken all Lisa and Diane's chips but they didn't. They were just having fun, and Lisa wound up adding $300 to her chip stack. The women saw an opportunity and went with it. Plus, they had a blast.

In a business situation, you can also use this to your advantage. When Jennifer first started working at a drug company, a key part of her job was to get the lawyers to approve advertising copy. She found it very difficult to deal with one particular attorney, whom we'll call Lewis Drake. He had been at the company 30 years and felt like he had seen it all. It was hard to talk to him, so she went to her female boss for advice. When she explained the situation to her Harvard-educated superior, she said, "Oh, when I have to deal with Lewis I wear my special Lewis Drake dress." Jennifer was perplexed. What her boss meant was that she had an outfit that showed just a little more skin than she usually wore, and that typically distracted Lewis enough to make him open to discussion on their ad claims.

Now, some of you will recoil when I say this, but it is reality. It's not necessary to be slutty or vulgar, but there is nothing wrong with discreetly using what you have. You would be foolish not to.

Playing Your Hand

- ♣ Use confidence and persistence to get you through a closed door.
- ♣ Take time for observation before action to get your best advantage.
- ♣ Stick up for yourself against a bully to win big.
- ♣ Bet against a Madonna Complex to get him out of your way.
- ♣ Rely on your feminine wiles to beat out a Mr. Romeo.

3
Location, Location, Location

Playing on the Button

In real estate, they say the three most important rules are "location, location, location," and in poker, it's "position, position, position." Your position at the table will dictate many of your actions. It will influence what hands you play and how much you bet. In a poker game, you're typically sitting at a table with ten people. The person on the dealer button, a round plastic disk that says "dealer" on it, is the last to act in the game, whether it is to bet, call, raise, or fold. The dealer button is passed around to the left every hand, so everybody has an equal chance of acting last. And in most cases, acting last has an important strategic advantage: You have the most information from your opponents before you need to make a move.

So if you're at a poker table and the first three people are betting and raising very aggressively, by the time it's your turn, you know you need very, very good cards in order to stay in that game.

Conversely, if everybody before you is just calling or folding, that indicates weakness, and you can play that hand and bet more aggressively. On the other side of it, if you are the first person to act—which in poker is called "under the gun"—and you're the first one to have to decide whether to bet or to check, you are pretty much playing in the dark. All you know are the cards you have in your hand. In the early position, if you have a pair of deuces, otherwise known as "ducks" or "twos," you will not usually play that hand, because it's the lowest pair you can have and you haven't gotten any information from betting patterns to let you know if the hand can be a winner.

However, if you have pair of deuces and you're in the last position and all the players before you pre-flop have folded or just called, projecting weakness, your deuces start to look a lot better. Conversely, if the players before you are betting aggressively and raising, you can safely assume your low pair is no good and should fold. The difference between the two scenarios is nothing more—or less—than position and the information you have based on your position that allows you to make a more informed decision.

Business negotiations follow the same tactical logic. The last person to speak in a negotiation is at an advantage. If somebody else speaks first, you know how much money they want. You know how much time they need. You know their interests. You know their priorities. You can make your offer with a lot more information, as opposed to you being the first one out there and perhaps being wildly off the mark. The opportunity to listen first and act later is an enormous strategic advantage.

Away from the Table

Speaking Last

The No. 1 manager under Fawn had asked for a private meeting with her. Fawn knew that Robin, who had been with the company for ten years, was underpaid compared to the newer manager hired into the company. It was often a problem to get the older managers' salaries on par with the new hires. Fawn was sure that Robin was coming in to ask for a raise, which she would have liked to give her, but there was a salary freeze. She was afraid if she did not increase Robin's salary, she would walk. The day of the meeting, Robin came in looking very serious. Fawn was nervous about losing her key employee. She spoke first and said, "I know you are making less than some of the new hires, but we are on a salary freeze and I cannot give you anything at this time even though you deserve it." Robin was stunned. She had come in wanting permission to take an extra week's vacation for her honeymoon. She had been unaware that she was making less than some of the other managers, so now she was angry and told her boss she expected to be brought up to her colleagues' compensation levels. Fawn had jumped the gun. She should have waited to see what her employee wanted before she spoke. She gave up the wrong information at the wrong time for no reason.

Acting last can work similarly in personal relationships. Vanessa was living with Stan, who always seemed to shut down and give her the silent treatment when they had an argument. She was always the first one to try to restart the conversation and get him talking. She would talk for twenty minutes about what was bothering her, and he said nothing about what was upsetting him. The conflict would die down, until the same pattern would recur.

Finally, Vanessa remembered a key teaching from her poker class the week before about the power of acting last. So the next time they fought she waited for him to open the conversation. It took several hours for him to bring it up but she finally found out from him why they were having the same fight over and over again. Letting him speak first, she was able to get the truth. In fact, he had a totally different take on the situation than she did and had been reluctant to speak previously because he didn't want another argument about their totally different viewpoints on the issue.

In successful dating relationships don't you find that, in many cases, women are the last to act? They wait to be asked out, they wait for a second phone call, and they wait to see if the guy is serious. In some ways, being reactive is an advantage because it leaves you less vulnerable. However, if you are not getting a read on the other players at the table or don't feel like you know where you stand in a relationship, you may want to put out a small "feeler" bet to test the waters or to give the other person a nudge. And you don't have to wait until you're in the last position to do this. In many cases, this is a way of acting before someone else while risking as little as possible. A feeler bet will help you gain some information about a person or situation. And you'll be able to gauge the other person's reaction, or at least get a feeling for how things are going.

Away from the Table
Putting out a 'Feeler' Bet

Shinikqua, an up-and-coming editor of a financial news website, went out with Ivan, a financial consultant, seven times and they never kissed. At the end of their first date, he waved goodbye to her as he got into a cab. She never thought she would hear from him again, but he texted her the next morning to say what a great time he had. Following their third date, he shook her hand in front of her doorman when he dropped her off. After the fifth date she finally got a kiss on the cheek.

She was racking her brain wondering what was going on. He took her to nice places and seemed interested in what she had to say. She went to his apartment to meet him, so she knew he wasn't married. Was he gay? Was he trying to exploit her for whatever privileged financial information she might have by virtue of her profession? Perhaps, but her gut told her he wasn't. Finally, after the seventh date, she had had it. She didn't want to seem too aggressive, but this was ridiculous, so she drew on her poker strategy and put in a "feeler bet" to see if she could get some information. She said, "Ivan, we have spent a lot of time together and I think it is unusual that we have not even kissed. I appreciate you taking things slowly, but this is abnormal." Ivan revealed that he was in a long-distance relationship that was in limbo and he wasn't sure where it was going. He thought he was being a nice guy by not have a sexual relationship with Shinikqua, but he was really being dishonest. Had she just let the relationship proceed at his pace, she may have been with him many more months before she found out the truth. Instead, she got the information she needed and could make a decision to move on.

Playing Your Hand

♣ Act last to have the best position.

♣ Put out a small "feeler bet" to gain insight and information from your opponents.

♣ Always remember that more information gives you more power.

4
Stop Betting Like a Girl

When you watch a poker game with both men and women at the table, you will see the men are significantly more aggressive than most of the women, even if the chips are fake and have no value. There is a very interesting phenomenon that occurs when we do a co-ed POKERprimaDIVAS® event. Typically, we give a prize to the top three chip holders when the tournament ends. That means if you do not finish in the top three, it doesn't really matter if you come in fourth or fiftieth. When we announce the last five minutes of the tournament, you will see the men starting to move all-in with their chips. But the women don't. They would rather have one fake chip left then lose everything. It happens all the time. And I always tell them the same thing: Stop betting like a girl. In other words, play to win—as opposed to avoid losing.

Women have a tendency to be more passive players, even very successful professional women. Frequently, they're calling stations, meaning they follow instead of taking the lead. As we've discussed in earlier sections, passive players rarely win big. If you're not aggressive at the poker table, I bet you're probably not as aggressive as you need to be in your personal or business life.

Women have been taught for hundreds of years that being aggressive is a negative quality or, worse, that it makes them a bitch. Aggression is not a dirty word or a non-feminine trait. Being aggressive doesn't mean being reckless or angry or mean. It's about acting boldly, taking advantage of situations that come to you, and focusing on a goal and going after it. For how long now have women been asked to apologize or to feel guilty for standing up for themselves and asking for what they want? A lot of our discomfort with being aggressive has to do with fear of "making waves" or causing trouble or appearing impolite. Many are also afraid that people will not like them. Aggression is actually intricately related to fearlessness. In poker, being both aggressive and fearless is enormously important.

Fear is an emotion that affects our entire state of being. Life is full of uncertainty and, with so much to protect, we typically find ourselves in a defensive crouch. We have mortgages, older parents, car payments, credit card bills, and jobs. Many of us have even more responsibilities with families and children to support. No matter how old or young you are, many of us become so scared of losing what we have that we don't go after what we truly want. We allow fear to paralyze our desires. We play it safe and hold on so tight to the status quo that we never experience the potential of what could be.

If you're not assertive in the workplace, you're not going to get what you want. If you don't ask for better assignments, you're not getting them. If you don't ask for a raise, you're probably not getting one, either. You have to take the initiative, because if you wait for others to recognize your worth or reward your competence, you're going to be waiting a very long time. You have to bet on yourself. As your knowledge of poker improves, you'll know when to make the bold plays that beat out the rest of the players at the table. You're not going to want to sit idly by and watch your chip pile diminish. If you are not betting, you're not being aggressive enough. And guess what? You're telling everyone else at your table that you think you have a weak hand.

Being aggressive also has its place in a romantic relationship. Without making your own moves, standing up for yourself and asking for what you want, you're stuck waiting for someone else to guess what you need. If you're constantly waiting for the other person in the relationship to see what they do and not really saying what you want, you're going to end up in an unfulfilling relationship. Aggression in a relationship is just a way of asking for what you want.

The other part of aggression is purpose: You need to play to win. A lot of women are afraid to lose at the poker table, in business, and in relationships. They force themselves to defend rather than advance. Playing "not to lose" sounds safe, but it's ultimately the most dangerous strategy of all because it guarantees that the best you can do is only mediocre. It will not get you what you want. To win, you need to know exactly what you want and you must be willing to risk failure to get it.

Instead, try turning it around and declare, "Okay, I'm going to get what I want at work, have a better relationship, and enhance my life." It's okay to put in all your chips. It's okay to take the lead. It's okay to be powerful. Playing to win requires a commitment to yourself that even if you fail, you will get right back up. Those who play to win know that success is not given to us. It is pursued with all the vigor we can rally. Impediments and struggles are part of life and only serve to make us appreciate our success. Obstacles are meant to be overcome. Fear is meant to be conquered. Success is meant to be achieved. They are all part of the game of life and the people who succeed play to win and never give up until the game is over.

In 2007, I played in a no-limit event in the World Series of Poker. There were more than 3,000 players. I only focused on keeping the chips I had. I was more concerned about getting knocked out too early than I was about winning. I had spent a lot of money buying-in and I wanted my chips to last. Well, you cannot win a poker tournament playing that way. You have to accumulate the big chip stack because chips are power. They are the tools or weapons you use to get what you want in the game—everyone else's chips. Just preserving my own chips but getting no one else's allowed me to sit there longer, but I wasn't going to walk home a winner. The winners at the table were always pushing the edge and were not afraid to get knocked out. They consciously went after the chips they needed, taking the necessary risks, while I just lost slowly. It took a while for me to learn that lesson.

Not every aggressive move is going to be successful. There are many times when you make an aggressive move, and someone comes "over the top" on you, and is even more aggressive. To defend against this kind of move, you need to know when to push back and when to back away. It's the same thing if you're in a business situation. You need to push as hard as you can, but there are certain times when you're going to have to back off, because your boss has a very different opinion, or you're the only outlying point of view on an otherwise united team. So, I do urge you to express yourself more and ask for what you want. Sometimes, however, you have to tone it down to get along.

Now, there are those at the poker table, as well as in your everyday life, who are too aggressive. They're so aggressive that they're actually reckless, and not very pleasant to be around. That doesn't make for a very good poker player, or for a very successful business person, or for a very stable relationship. Of course, there are exceptions. There are some very successful poker players who are extraordinarily aggressive, but luck plays an inordinately large role in their wins and every game is high drama. When they win, it's a seat-of-the-pants victory; and when they lose, it's an equally spectacular blowout. The ups and downs of these people are epic and have the tendency to drag friends, colleagues, romantic partners, and innocent bystanders along in their wake.

As a poker player, you want to be aggressive at the right time—namely, when you think you are in good position and have a chance of winning. To be ready when the moment comes, you need to be comfortable speaking up and taking charge. Women really have to practice doing that on a consistent basis. Start small and practice with little things. The next time you're in a restaurant, why not order for your table? If you're in a taxi cab, tell the driver the route you'd prefer to take. If you get resistance, push back. Think of it as going to a low-stakes poker table to get

Away from the Table
When Speaking Up Is a Matter of Life and Death

How many times have you left a doctor's office with unanswered questions because you were afraid to challenge an authority figure or even take up more of his or her valuable time? Diane tells a story of going to a doctor with vague but bothersome symptoms that lasted for more than six weeks. She knew her body and knew something was wrong. The doctor asked her a few quick questions and told her it was just stress. Diane was not a complainer and knew it was something else but did not want to push the issue. Finally, after another three weeks of feeling awful, she went back and asked that he do some more tests. Sure enough, she had an infection. She said it was one of the most difficult things she had ever done because she was afraid of being too pushy or aggressive. But having been bullied by men in her poker game, she had practiced pushing back and sticking up for herself. She was fortunate that this was not a life-threatening condition and that she found her voice before the infection became anything grave. Still, her experience made her wonder how many women might even now be battling serious illnesses just because they feared confrontation and meekly accepted a doctor's word as infallible.

some practice being aggressive before you move on to something that's bigger and more meaningful. And remember, being aggressive does not mean being argumentative or rude. You need to have a purpose and a goal in mind.

There are followers and there are leaders. Play poker and you will learn to lead. We talked before about a calling station, a person who wants to be in the action but never takes the lead. It's a very passive position. And again, it's a good way to not lose a lot, but it's not a good way to win. You're never really going to maximize your potential if you continue to be a calling station.

When you see beginner women playing poker, you typically see that most of them are calling stations. They tend to just follow what's in front of them, rather than set up what they want, go after it, and get it. If you continue to play poker and make a conscientious effort to ensure that you're not the calling station, that you're setting the tone and the pace of the game, you're going to see how this new, active stance affects the rest of your life in a positive way.

The other thing I see women doing all the time is apologizing when they win. Maybe they think it's cute or feminine. It's not. After you've played your game and you're rewarded with the win, don't feel guilty. You deserve what you have worked for. You rarely will see a man apologize to another man at a poker table for beating him. So once you go after what you want and you win, be happy, be gracious, but don't apologize for your success.

Away from the Table
The Joy of Taking Control

S usan came to a POKERprimaDIVAS® event, and took some follow-up lessons. She told us she had been in a relationship for three months, and pretty much had let her boyfriend set the tone. Susan didn't know where she stood. She didn't know if they were serious or exclusive. Because her boyfriend hadn't addressed these topics, they simply hadn't come up for discussion. Susan was not particularly satisfied with this.

One day, as she was contemplating her relationship, she recalled something that had happened at the poker table. She had been playing with somebody she couldn't get a read on who was pretty much a calling station, and wasn't taking any sort of initiative. So finally, when she was up against that player, she put in a large bet, just to get a reaction from him. He folded. She tried it again and he folded a few more times. In fact, almost every time she bet or raised him he folded his hand. From these experiences, she confirmed that he was a very tight player who would only call with a made hand.

That night, sitting across the table at dinner with her boyfriend, Susan decided to try the same strategy she had used at the poker table. She mentioned that she had a friend who had been dating someone for four months and just assumed they were seeing each other exclusively. She asked her boyfriend how he felt about it. He told her he thought it made sense and that he felt the same way. Susan had her answer. She was thrilled and realized that often the worst thing you can do is to do nothing, like the calling station at the poker table. Susan's poker experience allowed her to fearlessly find out what she needed to know.

Poker women take charge at the table and in their life. They are fearless. They do not suffer from gender-related guilt. So embrace your success and look forward to the next big win, whether it's in business, love, or personal fulfillment.

When you sit at the poker table with men, they often will trash-talk or antagonize each other. Just watch the games on TV and listen to Phil Hellmuth Jr. or Mike Matusow insulting each other or the other players. Typically you do not see the women engaging in this type of behavior. As a rule, women are overly concerned about whether they're being nice or hurting someone's feelings. Well, not everyone has to like you. From our earliest years, we're taught to be helpful and supportive people-pleasers. At the poker table, some women may not want to play hard against someone for fear of being too aggressive or unlikable.

Have you ever noticed that when you find yourself saying yes to everyone else, you often overlook your own needs? Suddenly you're not getting done what you wanted to get done. You lose your focus on what's in your best interest. Carry on that way long enough and you will likely begin to exhibit passive-aggressive behavior and ultimately melt down.

Away from the Table
Everyone Doesn't Have to Like You

Fran is a mother of three. She used to have a very intellectually stimulating job in the art world, but due to her husband's hectic traveling schedule, she decided to quit her job and stay home with the kids. Many of the other mothers in the neighborhood worked, so they would frequently ask Fran to pick up their kids from school if they were running late or to bring extra cookies for a temple bake sale. Sometimes, if a child was too sick to go to day care, Fran's house became the de facto day care center. At first, Fran had no problem doing all these things, but over time, the favors started to pile up. She no longer had time to garden or bike ride, and had even less time to spend with her own children.

Fran grew up in a family where she was taught that it was impolite and "un-neighborly" to say no, so she kept on driving and baking and babysitting for the other moms. When one mother asked Fran to watch her twin toddlers, Fran said yes, even though she was getting fed up. She put on a friendly exterior, but inside she was fuming. When the mother was 40 minutes late picking up her twin toddlers from Fran's house, it was the last straw. Fran blew up and angrily blasted her for putting so many burdens on her. The woman was in shock. Fran had always been so sweet! How would her neighbor know there was a problem when Fran always said yes with a smile?

When we try to please too many people all the time, we end up pleasing no one, least of all ourselves.

Playing Your Hand

- ♣ Be aggressive and ask for what you want. Don't make other people have to guess.

- ♣ Play to win, rather than to avoid losing.

- ♣ Save your most aggressive moves for when you're in the best position to get what you want.

- ♣ Control the situation rather than calling someone else's moves.

- ♣ Accept that not everyone will like you. It's more important to pursue your own happiness than to please others.

- ♣ Don't apologize for your success.

5
Perception Is Everything

Things are not always as they seem. As a poker player, it is your job to give everyone the perception that you have the best hand—whether or not you do. Many factors influence how people perceive you at the poker table, and gender is high on the list. When a woman walks into a poker room, typically the first thing a guy thinks is that she doesn't know how to play. In many cases that assumption can work to her advantage.

If you're playing cards with somebody who thinks you're a clueless amateur, you can get away with a lot more than if they're wary. You probably have a better chance of bluffing, because they don't think you have the nerve to be deceptive. You have a better chance to get them to fold when you put in a big bet, because they don't think you have the courage to make a move or risk a lot of money if you don't have a hand.

People perceived as very aggressive players often get more callers (people playing in a pot with them) than somebody who's only playing one hand an hour. People think aggressive players are bluffing more since they play like they always have a good hand.

On the other hand, players who don't engage in many hands are perceived as fearful, passive, and more easily bullied. Now, that may or may not be the truth. In fact, you might consider someone a passive player because she plays very few hands, but on the contrary, she may be a good, patient player who just hasn't been getting good cards. That's what happened when I was recently playing at the Borgata Hotel Casino & Spa in Atlantic City. I was getting horrible cards and kept folding my hands. I must have played two hands in two hours. When I finally entered a pot, a guy at the table said, "Oh, you must have finally gotten pocket aces." He thought I would only play with a made hand. A bell went off and I said to myself, "Okay, now I can start bluffing because everyone perceives me as being very tight, and when I bet they will most likely think I have a top hand and fold." I was able to use that strategy, bluff more than my fair share, and win several pots.

In poker, the more you play, the more you'll see how people try to toy with your powers of perception, often intentionally misleading you in an attempt to throw you off. Your job is to look beyond the obvious so you can get a clearer picture. That's what the poker players do. You may be surprised by what you learn.

Our initial perceptions are heavily influenced by how someone is dressed, the way they carry themselves, their choice of words and tone of voice, and their ability to make eye contact. People are sizing you up. You're sizing them up. But you have to get beyond the image to really understand what makes people tick, since looks can be deceiving. Do you know if the guy who wears a $5,000 watch is keeping up with his mortgage payments? Or if the woman in the new Jimmy Choos is three months behind on her credit card payments? Have you ever gone out with somebody who seems extraordinarily confident and sure of themselves, only to find out, after three dates, that they're one of the most insecure people you've ever met? Looking beyond image and discovering how people act is a much better indicator of character.

Away from the Table
Appearances Can Be Deceiving

Nancy's college friend Mallory seemed to have the perfect life. She lived in a stunning house, had two beautiful daughters, and a husband that made a seven-figure living. Mallory and her husband entertained frequently and were always attending school events holding hands. Every year the family sent out a holiday card with a beautiful portrait of the clan. Their life looked storybook perfect. Nancy, who was divorced, used to feel envious of Mallory. One day, Nancy walked into the pharmacy and ran into Mallory. They were chatting while waiting for their prescriptions when Nancy noticed that the pharmacist was putting two bottles of antidepressants into Mallory's bag. How could this be? What did Mallory have to be depressed about? It turned out she was lonely being married to a workaholic and she had fallen in love with her brother's best friend. She had been trying to end her marriage for years. It just goes to show you just never know what cards someone is really holding.

Emotional perception is another area where truth and reality are often unrelated. People can be feeling very differently inside than they appear to be. Katie is 5-foot-7, athletically fit, well dressed, well spoken, and has a great, outgoing personality. She works in a fast-paced company that is male dominated and she can roll with the best of them when she needs too. Katie is the poster child of self-confidence. This works well for her most of the time, from a professional standpoint. However, Katie also has a sensitive side that is not obvious to colleagues, new acquaintances, boyfriends, and even some family members. They don't see beyond her exterior. They perceive her as sturdy and resilient and, as a result, often say things that she finds hurtful. People just assume she's thick-skinned. But Katie strives to find the support and nurturing she sometimes needs. If people have the wrong impression, it's up to you to find out why and then adjust your behavior to have your needs met. Katie needs to be clear with people when she is hurt and speak up or she will continue to experience isolation and sadness.

The old saying "You can't judge a book by its cover" still rings true. But conversely, how you present yourself can go a long way toward impacting how people treat you. Think of the image of the prototypical poker player: male, overweight, cigar-smoking, 5 o'clock shadow, crude, uneducated. That stereotype no longer applies. Today, some of the best and brightest are being taught the game as part of the curriculum at Harvard Law School and MIT. Corporate titans are playing poker on a regular basis. Brian Haveson, former CEO of Nutrisystem, is a big player on the poker circuit. WSOP winner Chris Ferguson has a Ph.D. in computer science from UCLA, and Annie Duke, a finalist on Donald's Trump's *Celebrity Apprentice*, is a Columbia University graduate. Smart, attractive women are playing in world tournaments and garnering the respect of millions. In fact, I think women have improved not only the overall level of play, but the image of poker in general.

So what's the best way to find out people's perception of you? Talk to someone you know well and someone you don't. Compare their first impression of you and see if it fits with the image you are looking to convey. Note the distinctions between perception and reality. Remember that you can project the image you want others to perceive. The cards are in your hand.

Playing Your Hand

♣ Make sure you are projecting the image you want.

♣ Look the part, dress the part, and act the part and people will perceive the image you are trying to project.

♣ Look beyond the obvious to truly understand other people.

♣ Modify your image if you're not getting the results you want.

6
The Goldilocks Principle: Finding Your Game

There are many types of poker games. The one you are most likely to see on TV or in media is Texas Hold 'Em, currently the most popular variety. But Hold 'Em is far from poker's only game. To optimize your success, you have to understand which game is *your* game.

You might like Omaha, where you start with four initial pocket cards instead of two like you would in Hold 'Em. This means you have many more possibilities of combinations as the hand progresses, and so you tend to play more hands. Someone who likes to be in on the action more often might find Omaha a better fit.

Or you might be a Seven Card Stud player. Seven Card Stud requires a very good memory because four of the seven cards that you're dealt are dealt face up. As players fold and the cards are put away, you have to remember which ones you already saw on the table, and so a good memory gives you a significant advantage.

Or, at the other end of the spectrum, perhaps you're an iconoclast, someone who likes to break the rules. You might be good at a low-ball game like Razz or 2-7 Triple Draw. In these games, you turn the rules of poker on their head and aim to combine the lowest cards in the deck for what would traditionally be considered an awful hand. However, the nature of poker is that each round tends to *improve* your hand—and so a lowball game would be a poor fit for someone who gets easily frustrated and needs to conform to rules.

Similarly, you should choose your game in life based on what is best suited to your personality. A contract lawyer should enjoy desk work and attention to detail, while a trial lawyer should like to be on stage, using charisma as well as smarts to sway a jury. Perhaps your nurturing side leads you to become a teacher, or your ability to remain calm in high-pressure situations makes you a good airline pilot. If you're not happy doing what you do, if you don't feel right in your house in the suburbs, if your career leaves you unfulfilled, if you're doubting your marriage, then very likely you are in the wrong game.

The beautiful thing about poker, though—and about life—is that you can always modify your game. There's another kind of play around the corner, and it may be a better fit. With time and dedication, you can learn the new skills, practice a new game plan, and perfect a new strategy to make you a major player in a new field. It's not always easy to change your game. In fact, it is sometimes very painful. But it is always an option.

Away from the Table
Changing Your Game

How many people do you know who have gone into a profession because their parents wanted them to?

Terri came from a family with three generations of dentists, and from the day she could talk everyone primed her to carry on the family business. Without considering whether it would be a good fit or whether she would enjoy it, she went to dental school because it was expected of her. Terri hated the profession, and after practicing with her dad for fewer than three months, she knew she was in the wrong career. She started playing poker as a distraction from her work misery, and it became her only outlet for fun. As she recognized her poker strengths—for instance, she was a great cash-game player but did not have the stamina for twelve-hour tournaments—it dawned on Terri that what she was doing in life didn't play to her strengths. She needed to find and focus on things she was good at.

A dog lover, Terri had always been very good with animals of all kinds. Taking advantage of her natural skill, she decided she would go back to school and become a veterinarian. Her parents weren't happy about it, but more important, Terri was. She was finally playing in the right game.

Beyond the types of games, there are also different limits to these games, meaning different rules for how much you can bet. Even within Texas Hold 'Em, there are three major variations: There's No-Limit Texas Hold 'Em, Limit Texas Hold 'Em, and Pot-Limit Texas Hold 'Em—and they all require different skills. For example, in No-Limit Texas Hold 'Em, you always have the option of going all-in with as many chips as you have in front of you, which gives you a lot of opportunity to protect your hand and also to scare people away. With the ability to go all-in at any time, you take big risks but also force your opponents to potentially risk all they have in order to play with you. If you're good at making bold decisions and you're not afraid to risk all your money, a no-limit game is perfect for you. This is as much about personality as skill. You're going to be excited by this game's fast and furious action, and therefore feel more engaged. Conversely, when you're playing in a Limit or Pot Limit Texas Hold 'Em game, where there is a limit to the amount you can bet and you're not asking somebody to risk all their chips, it's a very different strategy. It's going to be much more difficult to bluff, because calling you is not necessarily cost prohibitive. The reward is not as big but neither is the risk.

So you need to find the game and limit that is right for you. If you want to excel at the top of your field, the stakes may include long hours, a lot of socializing with people you don't like, giving up family time. Know the stakes and the players so you can decide if you even want to play at that table. If you want to be in that game, be prepared to ante up. If you don't like the stakes, move on to the next table.

Beyond just the stakes, though, you need to choose the game that makes use of your strengths. I think a lot of people, particularly women, focus too much on fixing what they think they are doing wrong. That can often lead to a lot of wasted time and energy. So if you're playing a no-limit game and not doing well, that doesn't mean you're necessarily a bad poker player. It just means you're playing the wrong game. Instead of wasting hours of practice and study trying to get better at no-limit, why not turn to limit poker? Do you really need to be good at everything to succeed? I doubt it! If you wound up in the financial field and you're not a numbers person, maybe it's a waste of time to be hammering your head against a wall trying to transform yourself into a human calculator. Even if you were able to boost your math skills by an astonishing 50 percent, would it really enhance your career? Perhaps all that effort would be best spent on what you already do well. Your game might be in a creative field, where visual skills are more valuable, like graphic design. By focusing your time and energy on the game that's right for you, you're bound to reap a more substantial reward and avoid a lot of stress and self-loathing in the process.

When you watch a poker game, you'll see some of the players are true specialists. Some are really good playing pre-flop; others are better playing post-flop. Some players excel in cash games while others are better at playing in a tournament. Professional poker players understand the value of specializing. They identify their strength and that becomes their focus. They understand that it's much easier to improve what you're innately good at than it is to bootstrap your way to competence at something that's a struggle. If you try to be good at everything, you're most likely not going to be very good at anything—and you will be exceptionally frustrated.

I'm not saying that it's unwise to step out of your comfort zone on occasion. You absolutely should! Clearly, you can't grow if you never push your limits. You need to challenge yourself in poker and in life in order to take your game to the next level. The key, however, is to select the right areas and occasions to step out of your comfort zone.

I once met a very successful behavioral psychiatrist who said, "I can't tell you how many people tell me what they're not good at and ask me to help them try to fix it, when it's really meaningless to the rest of their life. They would be so much happier and so much more successful if they focused on their strengths."

It is not necessary to be good at everything. So when choosing your game, consider what personality and skill sets work best for you rather than trying to change your nature to fit the game. Consider the stakes you wish to play—are you a brazen high stakes bettor, or do you prefer to risk less with a smaller buy-in? Do you like the strategy of tournament play, where you're trying to knock out your opponents and be the last one standing, or do you prefer a cash game, where you can walk away from the table at any time?

Find a game that works better with your strengths, and with hard work and dedication you can become a master at the new game you choose. And remember that you have to enjoy the process. Nobody ever became a good poker player without loving the game.

Playing Your Game

♣ Move to a different game if you don't like the one you're playing.

♣ Know what stakes you're willing to play.

♣ Know what you're good at and enjoy and focus on that as much as possible.

♣ Be passionate about what you do.

7

Play the Players, Not Just the Game

When you're playing in a poker game, if you only focus on yourself, you will lose. If you only think about what cards you have or what hands you could possibly have after a flop, you are going to be in a losing situation most of the time. You need to see what others are doing, so you can take action intelligently.

When you're seated at the poker table and the other players are looking at their cards, you need to be looking at them. Look for facial reactions. Can you spot any tells? When a flop comes down, don't just figure how it helps your hand. You need to think: What did that do for me and what did it do for the person next to me? Poker is definitely a game about paying attention to both the rapid changes in action and to the people against whom you're competing. Poker rewards the observant.

Selena found out the hard way what happens when you don't pay enough attention to your competitors. At a tournament in

Atlantic City, she was playing in the best position, "on the button," and no one had raised before the flop. After the flop, there were two players left in the hand. Since she had the best position at the table and sensed weakness from the other players, she put in a substantial bet to try to steal the pot. However, another player then raised her and put her all in. Selena hadn't taken into consideration just how aggressively this man had been playing against only her, the one female at the table. Had she paid more attention to his style of play against her, she would have realized this wasn't someone she could bluff. He was targeting her as the lesser player and needless to say, she lost her chip stack.

Competition ought to be about bringing out your best, sharpening your skills, and putting them to the test. Unfortunately, women occasionally take competition to a more personal, destructive level. We internalize a professional conflict so that every win is a validation of self-worth and every loss is a devastating tragedy.

When women start to get competitive with each other, it sometimes gets nasty. We need to remind ourselves that competition is not personal. If somebody beats you in a poker game, it isn't because they want to crush you—it's because they want to win. If your boss is a little bit tough on you at the office, that's okay. That's at the office. That has nothing to do with you on a personal level.

Not everyone has the same appetite for competition. At the poker table and in life, you'll meet people who dread confrontation. They're going to be easy to beat, whether at the table, in the workplace, or in the social arena. Like it or not, life's most desirable prizes go to those who are willing to fight for them.

Conversely, there are some people who are so fiercely competitive that any conflict quickly escalates into an out-and-out war. Winning against this kind of opponent might require a full-scale battle and you'll need to gauge both your stomach for it and your interest in the prize. You might find that it's wise to pick your battles with care and engage only when the payoff is really worth it.

The interesting thing about competition is that your competitive arena can change anytime. In a poker tournament, as people begin to get eliminated, the tables start to get combined, so people get moved around and you wind up playing with new opponents at your table. The further along you go in the tournament, the more new players you will encounter. You therefore need to start the observation process all over again and analyze each new player.

The tournament process reminds me of the beauty business. When I worked in the health and beauty industry, we considered our competition to be the other big health and beauty companies. We were corporate snobs and barely acknowledged any of the smaller, niche players who mostly flew under our radar. But anyone who follows the beauty business now knows that many of the big product success stories are coming from the outlier companies, the ones that big organizations previously ignored.

I nearly dropped the remote when I saw Johnson & Johnson's® Neutrogena® make a superiority claim versus Proactiv®. A big pharmaceutical using an infomercial company's product as a benchmark! Totally unbelievable! Having spent the last several years working for one of the most successful infomercial companies in the industry, I have seen this phenomenon time and time again. Proactiv grew from a small start-up to close to a $1 billion brand— now it cannot be ignored. Similarly, look at Dr. Scholl's®, the gold standard in foot care. It launched its own version of the PedEgg®, another infomercial product that has sold more than ten million units. Nair®, the category leader in women's depilatory, has developed products to compete with Smooth Away®, which in less than one year quickly threatened Nair's long-term ranking as the No. 1 brand. These large corporations are smart to acknowledge that their competitive set has changed, and they adjusted their strategy accordingly. As a poker player, you must do likewise.

Your poker skills will teach you how to gauge your competition and also understand that it's about the game at hand, not about a personal attack. The poker table is a rich environment to learn that by paying attention to your opponents, you can better figure out a way to beat them and still walk away on a friendly basis. And a true PokerWoman™ will see these lessons as the gift that they are.

Playing Your Hand

♣ Pay attention not only to your situation, but to that of others around you in order to make the most informed decisions.

♣ Don't make conflict personal; whether you win or lose shouldn't ruin a relationship.

♣ Choose your battles wisely and pick the prizes you really want to go after.

♣ Recognize when your competitive set has changed.

8
Don't Fall in Love with Your Cards

Many poker players, especially beginners, make the mistake of falling in love with their cards. This happens for several reasons. Novices love having two cards of the same suit because they look pretty. They can have a king of hearts and a 4 of hearts, which will typically amount to nothing, but because the two red hearts look nice together, they get very excited about the hand. Or they will fall in love with their pair of kings, because it is the second best starting hand you can have in poker. However those kings (otherwise known as cowboys) may not be so lovely if an ace falls on the flop. But the hand most poker players fall in love with is ace-king, otherwise know in poker lingo as Big Slick or Anna Kournikova, because it looks good but never wins (I didn't make it up, I promise). That hand is one of the best starting hands you can have at the table and people tend to play it very aggressively pre-flop. But if there is a lot of raising pre-flop or when the flop comes down queen, 9, 6 of diamonds; that hand is not so nice anymore because you have nothing.

When you're playing your hand, if your good-looking cards no longer seem viable, you have to get rid of them. Don't get emotionally attached to them. Remember, looks can be deceiving. It's like a good-looking guy with no personality or no job. You have to be careful not to get too attached to your cards if all the signs tell you that they're not the winning hand.

From a business standpoint, have you ever worked on a project that you absolutely were in love with? Maybe you were assigned to a new product launch? You did all the market research, talked to all the right people and incorporated their advice. You looked at all the financial data and thought you had a real winner. You spent a year working on it and knew every conceivable aspect of that product. It felt like you were giving birth to something new and wonderful. Then, all of a sudden, you find out that another company is coming out with an item similar to the one you were going to launch. Their product poses hefty competition, with better claims, better attributes, or a better package. You go to your management team with confidence and proclaim, "We can overcome it! We're better marketers, we'll get better distribution, we're going to spend more money on advertising and promotion, and we can improve the formula. We can fix it, and make it better." While stalling management for more time, you give it three or four more tries, but you just can't get to where you need to be. You have to accept that the project is no longer what it was when you started and you have to ditch it. If you're too emotionally attached to the outcome, it's going to hurt you much more in the long run. You have to know when to get out and how to retain your objectivity. Or in other words, fall in love . . . but be smart.

Away From the Table
Knowing When to Fold

Andrea was responsible for managing a large cosmetics business. She thought it was the greatest product line there was. The brand had a long and valued history in the marketplace and consumers loved it. They could still recall commercials that were more than 20 years old. But the product line was not compatible with the newer, more natural looking, translucent products that people were buying, and sales were lagging. Well, Andrea had many strategic ideas about how she could change the perception of the brand. Unfortunately, the other team members did not see it that way and did not support her strategy. Because she believed in her ideas so much, she fought for them every step of the way and went against every person on the team. And although her strategy might have been viable in the long term, she couldn't get it implemented because she didn't have the support from the rest of the company. As a result, Andrea wound up alienating many of her coworkers and ruining her work relationships. She was too attached to the project and was playing the cards in her hand, not the people at the table.

Did you ever look at a house and fall in love on sight? Everything seems perfect and you just have to have it, so you put in a high bid, afraid to lose it. Then you do your homework and realize the comparable house down the block went for 20 percent less and the school system is not what you thought. You could have just made a very costly mistake based on your emotional attachment. The same thing happens at the poker table; you have to keep your hopes and affections in check to make sure you're making rational decisions based on the cards in front of you.

You'll also notice too many players that stay in a hand for too long. They stay in because they're stubborn, their ego is on the line, or they think they can outplay their opponents. They stay in because they're gamblers and they just won't get out or just to show how tough they are. Whatever the reason, it's a mistake.

Recognizing when you're beaten is critical to anything that you do. You may be in a bad relationship where the signs are clear: You're not getting along, you never laugh, you're not happy, you're constantly fighting, and the relationship is going nowhere. But before you end it, you count up all the "chips" that you've got riding on this relationship and the odds of it turning around. Perhaps you've spent a year with this person. That's a considerable investment of time, but what more could be done to affect the outcome? You could go to therapy alone or together, you could change your behavior or hope he will change his (very unlikely). You examine the options and do what is feasible. But at some point, you may say to yourself, "It's a loss and any more time spent on this is a waste. I'm not in the relationship that is going to make me truly happy." If that's the case, get out before you waste another year—or decade! It's like going to the poker table with $200 and losing $100 in the first fifteen minutes: Don't be afraid to get up and change tables. Cut your losses before you lose everything and move on.

Away from the Table
Cutting Your Losses in Romance

Mona was dating Danny, who was a well-educated, good-looking, fun-loving guy three years out of college. Everyone liked him because he had a charming personality and knew how to have a good time. The problem was that Danny was a big drinker. The evening started with beer and graduated to vodka and cognac. By the time midnight rolled around, Danny was in another dimension. Danny was a fun drunk the first few hours, but as the night wore on he would become loud, disruptive, and sometimes violent with others in the bar. Mona tried to dissuade Danny from drinking, but things just got worse. After several years of this behavior, Danny went to rehab to overcome his drinking problem. Within three weeks of returning from one of the most prestigious rehabs in the country, he started getting high again, but this time it was cocaine. Mona tried to fix him again and they did the same dance for another year. Then Danny managed to get off illegal drugs, but wound up spending $75,000 on watches and gadgets as shopping became his new drug of choice. He was who he was, and while the symptoms changed, he could not. Mona was in love with Danny and had invested five years with him, but she finally realized he could not change and she cut her losses, ending the relationship.

The workplace offers similar examples. You may be in a job for three years, and the people around you keep getting promoted. You're trying really hard and you speak to management about what they're looking for in order to promote you. They say, "We'll promote you after you do x, y, and z." And you do x, y, and z, and then they have another excuse, and another. You keep trying; they keep making excuses. It's just not happening. If that's the case, there's no need to stick around to hear the next excuse. You need to move on.

Often in poker, you know the price you're willing to pay to play your hand. If you love your pair of 10s, maybe you'll raise $25, but if someone else re-raises to $200, you'll know there are too many possible combinations that can beat you. So make sure before you play that you know at what point you need to walk away. Similarly, if you're in the middle of a business negotiation, or you're trying to put together a deal, determine your "walk-away" point before you spend an extraordinary amount of time, resources, and capital getting it done. This is sometimes the hardest, but always the most important pre-negotiation decision you must reach. It is not a decision to be considered later, in the heat of the negotiation. The deal must be approached calmly to better understand what each side needs to make it a win-win agreement. Then, if the other side becomes unreasonable and prevents an agreement from occurring, we must weigh the cost we placed on the deal in question. Do we really have a mutual relationship or merely one party taking undue advantage of the other? If the answer is unsatisfactory, you need to move on to the next.

With the stock market, sometimes you invest in something you thought was a sure winner, only to later realize that you have a dud. You can wait it out, hoping that something incredible will happen and it'll turn around . . . or you can admit that you made a mistake. It may be difficult to do, it may be hard to give up that money that's already invested, but when the signs are unmistakable, it's better to lose a little than to lose it all.

Folding Too Soon

While it is important to know when to get out, it is also important to not fold prematurely. The No. 1 mistake I see newbie poker players making is folding too soon. At the poker table, if nobody has bet before you, if nobody has put in any money, you have an opportunity to "check." All you're doing is letting the turn pass to the next player. When you don't have a lot of aggressive people at the table, and everyone checks, you wind up getting what is known as a "free card." So, why forfeit that possibility by folding? Beginner players think that if they have nothing they should just throw the hand away. Well, that makes sense if it is costing money to play, but if you can get in with no risk, why not do so? Sometimes you're better off just waiting it out, because no matter how good or bad a player you are, luck matters. And sometimes you get really lucky.

The same holds true in a job scenario. Sometimes you think you're working with somebody who seems destined to surpass you. She has a better education and gets along better with your supervisor, and you sort of give up, or fold prematurely. Why knock yourself out when that promotion is practically gift-wrapped and waiting on someone else's desk? That's a mistake a lot of people make. They're afraid of being rejected, or afraid of not getting what they want. Rather than just stepping it up a notch and trying to improve their standing, they give up.

I see this all the time in the way women approach relationships. If a relationship isn't going exactly as you see fit, it can be tempting to "cut your losses" by ending it. Sometimes, however, you're better off waiting it out and learning how to love through the rough patches. There will always be tough spots and periods of stress during any relationship that you can use as both learning and strengthening opportunities to allow the relationship to grow. It's not a question of waiting until you put too much good money after bad, or until you've wasted too much time. Sometimes things deserve a chance to see if they get better.

In a poker hand, let's say you're on a draw, and somebody is betting aggressively before you. Well, before you fold, you need to assess the impact of "what ifs." What if your opponent actually has weaker cards? What are the possible hands your opponent might have? How much can you win and what is the payout? Think through the different scenarios before you decide to give up.

Knowing when to fold or when to stay in the game is a skill that comes with experience. Sometimes it's better to just fold and go on to the next hand or the next relationship or the next job, but be careful not to fold prematurely because if you've invested time, effort, and money into the current situation, it could be to your advantage to wait it out. However, if you have very little invested, and you're pretty sure the next thing that's coming up is going to be a better fit, then yes, you do want to fold. Make sure you are acting from the facts and not out of emotion. Managing emotions is absolutely critical to clear thinking. Sometimes, while we may really believe we are acting rationally, we are in reality just following the direction dictated by our inner fears.

Playing Your Hand

♣ Don't let emotional attachment cloud your judgment.

♣ Recognize when you are beaten.

♣ Beware "love at first sight." Looks can be deceiving.

♣ Don't be afraid to cut your losses, even if you've made an investment.

♣ Don't fold out of fear.

9
Talking Trash

Sometimes your fellow poker players will start coaxing you, making jokes about you, or be out and out insulting you. In poker, it's called trash-talking and is a tactical maneuver to distract you and throw you off your game. Your opponents will talk to you while you're trying to make a decision, try to guess what cards you have in your hand, tell you to fold because you're beaten, or do something odd and unexpected to confuse you. Trash-talk is actually very effective, and it's perfectly legitimate. You're allowed to trash-talk and distract your competitors as long as you don't reveal what is in your hand.

At a poker tournament for a children's charity, there was great example of trash-talking. One of POKERprimaDIVAS'® students, Lori, was playing. Of about 90 people, maybe 15 were women. Lori is a confident, outgoing woman, but she was new to the game. She had only been playing for about four months, but she decided to play in the event and see what it was like to play something other than her home game.

Lori did an outstanding job. She was playing her hands well, and fortunately, she was also getting good cards. After about three hours of play, she made it to the final table. Lori was the sole female up against nine men, all of whom had been playing for several years. It was apparent that several of the guys at the table knew each other. Lori was playing aggressively and she was winning. She was not folding a lot of hands—when you get down to just a few players, you can be more liberal with the hands you play because there is less competition. She was betting aggressively and within about 30 minutes, she had knocked several men out of the tournament.

The guys were not happy about getting knocked out by a woman. So, at about midnight, with the evening drawing to a close, there were three people left: Lori and two men who happened to be friends. That's when the relatively quiet, polite game took a turn. The two men started to talk to her when they would make a bet. They would throw in a bet, and as she would contemplate her next move, they would talk to each other, comment on her play, and guess out loud what cards she had in her hand, trying to knock her off her game.

For the first couple of hands, they were successful. They intimidated her, and she threw in her cards. I happened to be at the tournament and came by to give her a pep talk, explaining to her exactly what they were trying to do. So, for the next couple of hands, she just ignored them. They continued to trash-talk, and she continued to ignore them. In fact, she started trash-talking with me, to put them off their game. Sure enough, Lori won the tournament and two tickets on JetBlue to her choice of destination anywhere in the United States!

Trash-talking is not just confined to the poker table. It's far more common in everyday life than we may be aware of. Have you ever worked with someone who tried to put you on the spot in front of other people? Or been the object of someone's negative joking, when each comment feels like a sharp jab at you? Or there's the person who pretty much ignores you, talks over you, talks to others when you're talking, or makes pointed comments about what you say. Then of course, we have the colleague who says, "Look, I've been doing this for years and when you've been around as long as I have, maybe you'll pick it up." They're usually the ones who take your ideas and pawn them off as their own. More trash-talk designed to throw you off your game. When someone does it to you, you have two choices. You can ignore it—which is a talent that takes time to develop—or you can give it right back to them because once again, the trash-talker is a bully, and there's a lot of bullying going on at the poker table, in the workplace, and in life in general.

You'll even see trash-talk in romantic relationships. Some couples have a loving banter, but others can be downright nasty. A man might say something like, "Doesn't that dress look a little bit tight on you?" or "Have you started eating pasta and candy again?" Or my personal favorite: "I noticed you're looking a little bit tired lately." Many women hear these kinds of "observations" and are rocked by them. After all, they originate with someone who's supposed to care about them. Why would someone who loves you say something critical if it weren't both helpful and necessary? The more insecure the person, the more likely they are to use trash-talk to give themselves an advantage over someone else. Don't let them get away with it! Whether you're at the poker table or your kitchen table, the best way to deal with trash-talk is to ignore it and concentrate on playing your best hand.

Away From the Table
Tuning Out Trash Talk

Karen, a thin, stylish, and very attractive woman had been dating Doug, whom she met on a blind date, for about three months. Doug was okay-looking but could stand to lose about twenty pounds. He dressed very well and was conscious of appearances. After a long lunch in Soho one afternoon, Doug turned to Karen and said, "If you keep eating like you did today, you might not fit into those pants anymore. You better be careful." Now, coming from a guy carrying at least an extra twenty pounds, this was a pretty nervy statement. So why'd he launch an unprovoked attack about Karen's weight? Perhaps this had something to do with the fact that Karen had just watched him polish off a huge bowl of rigatoni carbonara. He was probably feeling like a pig for devouring lunch and he was going to make her feel bad because of it. That relationship lasted another two months, but in my opinion, it ended right after lunch.

It's not just the men in our lives who trash-talk. Women resort to their own brand of negativity with other women, often called "cattiness." Sometimes we need to reevaluate the girlfriends in our lives. Women's friendships are deep and complex and can be the closest, most supportive relationships we have. Yet, there are times when you see the caller ID of a particular girlfriend, you want to run and hide. If you have a friend who continually tries to cut you down—whether by discouraging your goals, saying you can't do something, finding fault with all your relationships, even criticizing your appearance—then perhaps her trash-talking shows you that she's not a real friend, and you should cut her loose. But more frequently, you'll find a woman's trash-talking just needs to be ignored, exactly like it does at the poker table.

In order to live the life you want and accomplish the goals that you set for yourself, you need to stay focused and surround yourself with people who are supportive of you and your aspirations. But when others do try to sway you, you can't let them throw you off your game. Trash-talk exists, whether we like or not. When you learn to tune out the trash-talk at the poker table, you'll also find yourself better able to focus on your true objectives and tune out the negativity that may be affecting your spirit and success.

Playing Your Game

- ♣ Tune out trash-talk.
- ♣ Trash-talk is a bullying tactic, so you need to either ignore it or push back the bully.
- ♣ Don't take trash-talk personally.

10
Why You Need a Little Mystery

Poker players look for something called a "tell" when they're playing with their competitors. A tell is typically a nonverbal cue that will give you an indication as to whether somebody has a good hand. Look around the poker table and you'll see some people move their chips in very quickly when they have a good hand. (Of course, some people move them in very quickly to *pretend* they have a good hand.) Some people will start chewing their gum very hard if they're nervous. They might start shaking their leg or shifting around uncomfortably in their seat. They might start toying with their drink or eyeglasses. You may see a vein in their temple start to throb. There are numerous tells, and there are numerous books written on how to spot and decipher them.

The bottom line is that tells are valuable insider information that you can only glean from close observation. When poker is played well, it is largely a nonverbal game. The significant information is not so much what people say, it's what they don't say. It's what they do, how they cock their head and move their eyes.

To avoid giving away these valuable clues, many poker players take unusual precautions. Some wear sunglasses, so you can't read their eyes. Phil Laak, nicknamed "The Unabomber," wears a hooded sweatshirt that nearly covers his entire face. But if you're playing with less seasoned players, you're unlikely to encounter such extreme measures, and the table is rife with opportunities to test your people-reading skills.

Try it on your own. Pick one or two people at the table and see if you can pick up any tells from them. We all reveal something about ourselves through our body language. Check how physically close someone is to you. The closer they are, the warmer their opinions are of you. The farther away that someone is, the less they care. Watch for head position. Overly tilted heads are either a potential sign of sympathy, or if a woman smiles while tilting her head, she is flirting. Alternatively, the person might be trying to convince you of their honesty. A lowered head indicates a reason to hide something; a cocked head means that they are confused or challenging you, depending on the set of their eye, eyebrow, and mouth.

The eyes divulge so much. Liars will repeatedly look at you and look away a number of times. You can actually learn specifically how to observe behavior to judge whether someone is lying. Looking to the side means that the person feels guilty. When you ask somebody where they were, look very carefully at the direction they turn their eyes. If they look to the right, they are recalling an event or a memory, meaning that they are telling the truth. However, if they look to the left, they are making something up. Interrogators look for these tells all the time.

People with crossed arms are closing themselves to social influence. The worst thing that you can do to people with crossed arms is to challenge them in one way or another, no matter how they react. This annoys them. Though some people just cross their arms as a habit, it may indicate that the person is reserved or uncomfortable with their weight (therefore trying to hide it). If someone rests their arms behind their neck, they are open to what is being discussed and interested in listening more. If they are playing or fiddling with their hair (a woman may twirl a lock of her tresses around a finger), they are feeling self-conscious, flirting, or possibly uncomfortable. If someone is biting their lip, they are anticipating something or holding back.

Clearly, being able to read other people's unconscious tells is a skill that comes in handy in other scenarios. If you have a boss who isn't very good at communicating verbally, you pick up little signs. For example, when he needs to share bad news, he sits far back from you when at his desk. Or the other salesperson who's been trying to horn in on your territory tends not to sit next to you in a meeting. These are tells that let you know how the other person feels about you.

There are even tells in a relationship. If you're out with somebody and they're looking into your eyes, and they hold your hand, even if they're not saying anything, you get an idea of how they feel for you. We had one student, Beth, who said she had been dating someone who didn't speak much about their relationship. In fact, he just didn't have much to say in general, but when they were out together, he was always caressing her hand, smiling at her, and would sit as close as he could. After about six months, he brought up getting married! Beth was in shock because he had never spoken about anything that even came close to those feelings, but in hindsight she said she could feel it from his tells.

Relationship tells are very important to look at—whether they're positive, encouraging signs or negative, red flags. Somebody may say the most wonderful things to you, but their body language may say something entirely different. Indeed, body language can tell you if a car salesman is lying, or if your kids are hiding something from you. If someone is telling you how wonderful you are, or lavishes praise on your work, but can't look you in the eye, that's an obvious tell that something is amiss. Dig deeper. Do they have their hand in front of their mouth when they're speaking, almost as if they're trying to keep the words from spilling out? These could also be tells that indicate that they're not telling you the whole truth.

Although most tells are nonverbal, that does not mean that chatter, which is relatively scarce at the table, is unimportant. Usually if there is talk, it's being used offensively, to distract you, or flush out one of your tells, and feel you out. Some poker players will start talking to you in the middle of the game just to see if you're comfortable talking to them. You'll see this tactic a lot on the professional games broadcast on TV.

While you're trying to read others' tells, be mindful of your own. You might be giving away far more than you realize. Do you consistently make eye contact when you speak or does that depend on whom you're talking to and what you have to say? Do you stand unusually close or far away from others? What about your voice? Do you speak in a calm, even tone even when you're very excited? Are your hands crossed in front of your chest? You have to monitor others' tells, but you have to make sure your tells are saying what you really want to communicate!

Away from the Table
Monitoring Your Tells

Rebecca could not understand why the people in her office never invited her to lunch or to any of the after-work activities. She always greeted them in the hallway and e-mailed them cute stories. She was hip, well-dressed, and very smart. She thought she was being very friendly and personable. What she didn't know was that her nonverbal cues—"tells"—were anything but friendly. She sat in meetings with her arms crossed, she was always taking notes, and she rarely smiled. People thought she was unfriendly and aloof. Rebecca had no idea. Finally, one day, she was at a lunch meeting in the conference room and was sitting next to someone she had little personal interaction with before. The two laughed a lot and had a really good conversation. At the end of the meeting, the woman said, "I can't believe how much fun you are, you always look so serious!" Rebecca was shocked, but now she understood.

Ask a friend for an honest assessment to read your body language. Ask someone who isn't a friend—and remember to take whatever they have to say as valuable, constructive criticism. When you've identified your own particular tells, you can choose to make them work for you. There are times when you want to deliberately let a tell "slip" in order to deceive your opponents. Misinformation is a potent offensive weapon.

Away from the Table
Using Tells to Manipulate

Suzy worked in a very male-dominated office in Chicago. She had a Wharton MBA and was very attractive. Her father was the former CEO of the company for which she worked. Suzy recognized that her credentials and attributes had the potential to intimidate colleagues and keep potential friends and allies at arm's length. So Suzy made a conscious effort to be gregarious, tossed her hair a little too often, and nodded her head in agreement when anyone was talking. When people who knew Suzy's background met her in person, they were thrown off by her tells. She was less intimidating and threatening than they expected. This was precisely what Suzy wanted to achieve. When she went into a negotiation, she wanted people to think she was sweet and a little goofy, because that made them let down their guard and made it easier for her to negotiate and get what she wanted. Her tells were carefully crafted just the way she wanted them to be. She was in control.

Away from the Table
Tells in Relationships

One night in New York I went out to dinner out with Joanne and Carl, who had just gotten engaged. I had known Joanne for many years and was happy she found someone she loved. Carl spent almost the whole night telling the eight of us at the table how he and Joanne met, how much fun they had together, how much they laughed, and how beautiful she was. He was nonstop. He held her hand and poured her water and wine when her glass was empty. He fed her bites of his food and wiped her mouth (I swear) after she took a bite. He was so sweetly attentive that it bordered on saccharine. However, when Carl got up to go to the men's room, my boyfriend noticed that he was ogling every woman in the restaurant, especially the young ones. On his way back to the table, he stopped to talk to the hostess and put his arm around her. He was gone for almost fifteen minutes. Back by Joanne's side, he was back in character as the adoring fiancé. Then, a few minutes later, when Joanne excused herself, his eyes started darting around the room. When she got back to the table, Joanne started to tell everyone a story about a project she was working on, and Carl started yawning. He clearly had no interest in what she was saying. When we left the restaurant, we discussed how confused we were by Carl. His actions and his words were a total disconnect. I didn't say anything to Joanne, but six weeks later, she called me to say the engagement was off.

Poker is the ideal venue for honing your nonverbal observation skills. Think of the table as a lab for dissecting the words, movements, and deeds of your fellow players to reveal the deeper meaning of their intentions. In "real life," your skill with tells will serve you well. Observe yourself. What our subconscious is thinking and feeling is not always obvious to our conscious mind.

Playing Your Game

♣ Pay attention to people's nonverbal cues—what is not said is as revealing as what is.

♣ Note your own tells and make sure they are the ones you want to communicate.

♣ Manipulate your tells to your advantage.

11
Motivation: Yours and Theirs

"If you can't identify the sucker at the table, it's you."

Figuring out why people do what they do can provide you with critical information. There are some people at the poker table who want nothing more than to win money. There are other people at the poker table who are just there for the action; they want to be in the game. They don't care if they win or if they lose, they just want to be in the thick of any situation and they love the heady rush of adrenaline that comes with it. Then there are those who come to the table just for the social interaction. I find that there's more of a social atmosphere when women are at the table, whereas men are far more interested in competing and winning. The person who's just there to be social doesn't care if they lose money to you. If it costs them a few bucks to get an evening's worth of entertainment, they are happy. So you're going to play differently against them than against the person who is there strictly to take your cash.

Understanding who's playing and why will help you plan your playing strategy. Some people eat because they're hungry and some people eat to calm anxiety. Some people talk because they want to be recognized, and some people ask questions because they want to make someone else look stupid. Knowing why they are asking a question can help you shape the answer. Effective leaders instinctively question the motivations in the personal interactions they have. Building this instinct is not that difficult, but it does take practice. Most people have an instinct for understanding why. So, next time you have an interaction of any sort, ask, "What's their motivation?" or "What are they trying to accomplish?" For example, some people are motivated by the need to feel powerful. Others are motivated by money. Understanding people's basic motivations offers you a key advantage in satisfying their needs, and they in turn will be more likely to satisfy yours.

From a business standpoint, if you have a boss who's motivated by keeping everybody happy, you're going to behave differently than if you have a boss whose sole purpose is to get promoted, or whose sole motivation is to outperform her peer. Some bosses only care about keeping their jobs and avoiding friction or any sort of confrontation in the organization. So the better you understand other people's motivations, the better you can adapt and decide if you even want to play in that arena. If you're working for somebody who doesn't like to make waves and you're an innovator, it's not a good match for you. Conversely, if you're working for somebody who is motivated strictly by getting ahead and wants to work

Away from the Table
New Players, New Strategy

Ariel went to work for a small company after being employed by a corporate giant for ten years. After about a month at her new job, she was asked to put together a marketing plan to launch a new venture. Her boss asked her to have it done in four days. Ariel went crazy. She used to have two months and a big staff to help her undertake such a plan, and she wasn't sure how she would get it done. She finally put together a detailed plan and scheduled two hours with the CEO and team to review. The day of the meeting, she began the presentation as she would have at her old company, with a very detailed grid of what was happening in the marketplace. She spoke for about five minutes before the CEO interrupted her and asked what she had planned for the following year. But Ariel had about 10 more charts to review before she got there. Unfortunately, her new boss had the attention span of a flea and stopped listening. He again told her he was only interested in the plan for 2010. She fast-forwarded over her pages of supporting documentation—pages that represented many hours of hard work. Her boss thanked her and left the room. Ariel was pissed off that she had spent all that time working on a presentation that her boss did not have the courtesy to sit through.

Unfortunately, Ariel had not gauged her audience. She went by what had worked in the past. At her previous employer, where quantity and thoroughness was valued, it was common to spend hours reviewing a plan. She forgot to adapt to what her new boss wanted. Short and to the point. He was happy if you could get him in and out of a meeting in twenty minutes. Next time, Ariel was much more concise.

24/7 and you're more interested in quality of life and spending time with your kids, that's not a good match, either.

Whether at the poker table, dinner table, or conference table, you sometimes need to adjust your play to the personalities of others. In a relationship, understanding motivation is particularly important, because everybody comes into a relationship with their own baggage. A recent fight with a spouse or stress over a sick friend could have a strong influence on someone's behavior or even their basic motivations. You may have one idea about how the relationship ought to flow, but when you're with a new partner, it's helpful it look at their situation and motivations to understand how the relationship is likely to evolve. Each situation is different. Some people respond to threats; others would walk away in a second from any confrontation. Some people are open books who after five minutes in your presence will tell you everything about themselves. Others seem to think all information is on a "need-to-know basis" and refuse to reveal anything more personal than name, rank, and serial number. It doesn't mean one way is better than the other; it just means you can't get anywhere using the same tactic on everyone.

The better you know and understand whom you are playing with, the better you are able to adapt your behavior to get what you want. At the poker table and in your personal life, knowing what people want and why they are there is going to help you decide if you want to be in a situation, and how to play once you are. Look at how the other players interact with each other to observe other people's motivations. Test your assumptions and see if they hold up. But remember that poker is a game that is constantly changing,

Away from the Table
Understanding Motivation in Romance

Diane had not been in a relationship for more than a year and was anxious to meet somebody special. When she finally did, she was hoping the relationship would move forward quickly. After all, she had waited so long for the right person that she assumed when he finally came along the two of them would run—not walk—into the sunset. That's not the way it happened when she met Chris. While the relationship was indeed progressing, it was at a much slower pace than she wanted or ever had experienced before. Chris had recently come through a messy divorce after 25 years of marriage, had twin daughters, and was pretty gun-shy about getting involved again. Typically, if the relationship wasn't going the way she wanted, at the pace she wanted it, Diane would have ended it. But she understood that Chris had to be more cautious because of what he had been through. And she did see evidence of progress in the relationship, although it was slow. So she decided to be patient and give Chris more time to catch up with her emotionally. During the next year, he did exactly that. Had Diane not looked at the situation, and had she not understood whom she was playing with, she would have prematurely ended something that turned out to be very good for her.

so what motivates someone now may be completely irrelevant later. As a result, be ready to adapt your understanding of what motivates each person as the game goes along.

Playing Your Game

♣ Determine the motivation of the players best suited to your style of play.

♣ Motivations may not always match but they can be complementary.

♣ Adjust your strategy based on your understanding of someone else's motivation.

12
Making Your Move

As the New York State lottery once said in its commercials, "You've got to be in it to win it." And in poker, you can't sit idly by and wait for the perfect situation to occur. Sometimes you may have to guess, but at the very least, you need to do something to make the action happen. In poker, taking action can mean several things: You might passively gather intelligence by paying attention to everybody at the table, plotting your next move. Or you might put in a small bet (a "feeler bet") to get a read on everybody and gather additional information, to make a more informed choice. But the one thing you should not do at the poker table is wait for certainty.

You can't just wait and see what happens because very passive players are never going to get what they want, whether they're at the table or elsewhere. If you're looking for a promotion at work and there's an opening, ask for it, even if you're not sure you're the most qualified candidate. It certainly can't hurt to ask and you might be pleasantly surprised. That's what happened to Heidi. She was working at the largest food company on the East Coast when a divisional VP spot opened up, a very rare occurrence at this organization. There were about six or seven people who were considered forerunners for the job. Heidi was talking to a friend one day who asked her if there had been any decision about the new VP spot yet. She replied that there was no news. Her friend, a very aggressive poker player, said, "Why don't you just ask for it?" Heidi thought she was nuts. Why should she have to ask? Didn't they already know she wanted it? Could she possibly influence their decision? Her friend said "You have nothing to lose and besides, if you are not happy with the answer, at least you know where you stand and can start networking." So Heidi mustered up her courage and went in to see the divisional president and put in her pitch for the position. When they were done with their conversation, he said, "I am so glad you came in here and told me you want the job. It shows you are assertive and know what you want. That's a sign of great leadership." Three weeks later, Heidi was the new VP.

A huge factor in hesitation to act is fear of doing the wrong thing, or making a mistake. There are two ways to deal with this. One is to imagine that worst-case scenario that's really holding you back (like embarrassing oneself—that's a big one for most of us) and say to yourself, "So what?" People embarrass themselves all the time; in fact, if you watch popular and successful people, you'll see that they mess up too, but more important, they rebound from their mistakes. They joke about it, or they make fun of themselves, and they immediately accept that they're human. After spending five months in jail, Martha Stewart rebounded immediately with a high-profile new television show. In early episodes, she even joked about the food in jail and how she finally started using a microwave. That she was able to put her mistakes behind her so successfully won her a whole new audience. If you make a mistake, it's *not* the end of the world. In poker, losing one hand just allows you to prepare for the next.

The other way to handle fear of making a mistake is to consider what will happen if you don't act. Remember that hesitating means *not* acting, and not acting has its own consequences. Don't want to talk to that guy because you're worried you'll put your foot in your mouth and ruin your chances with him? Well, you might, and that's okay; life will go on. Or, you might win him over. You never know! But, if you *don't* act, you guarantee that nothing will ever happen. How can sparks fly when you won't even come face-to-face with him? Do you really want to just wait for him to do everything?

In any situation, including romantic ones, it is often better to be proactive than reactive. A lot of women are more comfortable waiting for a man to make the first move. They'll wait to see what a particular suitor does and try to gauge his intentions. That's okay at the beginning. However, if you're not getting the right read from sitting back, and you're not picking up the tells that provide you with the information to inform your next move, you're going to have to do something. Ask a question, even if you may not get the answer you want. Take the initiative—because if you just wait, you may be wasting your time. Sometimes, a fast "no" is better than a long, drawn-out "maybe." If you are afraid of the answer, you will be paralyzed with inaction. As I have heard numerous times from Executive Coach Laura Nash, "When we are fearful, we are sabotaging our dreams."

Away from the Table
Asking the Uncomfortable Questions

One of our students, Roberta, was dating somebody for about a year whom she really liked, but she couldn't tell if her beau wanted something long-term. She didn't want to rock the boat. What if he thought she was too clingy? What if she scared him away by appearing too needy? So instead of saying anything, she just kept going along. Finally, after about another six months of patiently waiting for a sign, she said to herself, "Well, you know what? Either I'm going to waste another year like this, or I'm going to find out how he feels and what his intentions are." And that's what she did. Lo and behold, her boyfriend's response was a pleasant surprise. He had actually been waiting for her to bring up their relationship because he was afraid to himself and he wanted to take it further. Now she knew where she stood. You just can't wait, sit back, and let it happen to you. You have to make it happen or find out why it's not and move on.

Of course, action alone is sometimes not enough. Success in poker and life depends on timing. In poker, you don't want to start betting against somebody who seems to be winning every hand. That's not the time for you to take action. The time for you to take action is when you are having a surge of good luck, or when you're facing a weaker, fearful player or somebody who's having a bad run. So assess the situation and pick the right time. Don't go in and ask for a raise when the company is just reporting two bad quarters. Don't ask your boyfriend where you stand in the relationship after he's just been fired or after he has just signed his divorce papers. As you play more and more poker, you'll notice that your sense of timing will improve in all aspects of your life. It's a skill that requires you to pay attention to others as you evaluate the situation correctly. If you feel the time is right, take action. If not, fold and return, emboldened to play another hand.

Becoming a person who takes action takes self-confidence. Getting out in the world, having new, different experiences (playing in a poker tournament, for example) helps you learn to cope with new situations, which helps you become a more decisive person. As you broaden your horizons and open yourself up to new experiences, you will be more certain of what will happen in different circumstances. And when you're more certain and confident, you're more able to take action in all aspects of your life.

The Role of Patience in Taking Action

The old saying "patience is a virtue" is critical for your survival in a poker game. As important as it is to take action, it's also very important to learn to take your time. A really good poker player will only play about 20 percent of the hands she is dealt. You may sit at a poker table for two hours and play only one or two hands. As a beginner, you'll find all this "downtime" very frustrating (even though, as mentioned earlier, you're supposed to be using this time to study the other players), because when you first start the game, all you want to do is play cards. You don't want to sit there. But you don't want to play bad hands, either. In life, as in poker, we are dealt more than one hand. The trick is to get in at the right time, but don't be discouraged if the first few hands don't go your way. Eventually you will get to play the right hand and your patience will be rewarded.

Your patience is tested daily—at the supermarket, in traffic, and don't even get me started on the airlines. We normally don't have a choice, unless we want to stew and be in a bad mood for the rest of the day. But don't confuse patience with complacency. I'm not advising you to sit back. You do need to take action and to participate. Part of waiting for your moment is the knowledge that when it comes, you'll be ready to grab it. But if you've wasted all your cards, chips, and credibility because you didn't wait until the conditions were right for you to play the best hand of the night, you'll be kicking yourself later.

Often, if you've just played a bad hand, you're mentally off kilter. You're beating yourself up and antsy to get back in the game to refight the battle you just lost. But like a rebound relationship that is ultimately unfulfilling, impatient play will result in more unwise moves. The consequence of this downward spiral is even more impatience and decreased mental acuity. It's like that girlfriend who instantly falls in love every day. Impatience leaves little room for our better instincts and skills.

Away from the Table
Don't Be in Such a Rush

A 41-year-old journalist, Krystal was always complaining that she wanted a boyfriend. Her friends coaxed her to try online dating. She finally caved in and signed up on one of the more popular sites. She met one guy, but that went nowhere. Then she met another. They spent hours talking on the phone before meeting one evening. Their first encounter was spent at a candlelit outdoor cafe and they talked for hours. He shared his excitement with her about his upcoming trip to China to study Eastern Medicine. He kissed her passionately good night. Krystal was in love. It was all she could think about. She had trouble getting her stories into the newspaper on time. When she did take the time to talk to her friends, all she could talk about was this fabulous guy. She invited him for long weekends, baked special breakfast treats, and suspended her volunteer activities. But the guy was leaving the country in a few weeks. She kept hoping that he would invite her to visit him in China and that their relationship could weather the time and distance until he returned. Alas, a week before he was leaving for China he broke it off with her, frankly telling her that he never planned for the relationship to go anywhere. She was devastated. Had she not been as impatient to get a boyfriend, she might have spared herself the pain of getting her heart set on a relationship that from the start looked like it was going nowhere.

In poker, perhaps the best example of true patience can be found playing a tournament. A big tournament can go on for days. It's like the Tour de France or a 26½-mile marathon. You have to stay in it to win. It requires infinitely more patience than your Friday night home game. It can be hard to keep focused for that length of time and the impatient player will start making poor calls or bets.

If practiced with diligence, patience is as much an activity as any endurance sport.

Playing Your Game

♣ Make a move to increase your chance of winning.

♣ Avoid fear of failure; the worst thing you can do is nothing.

♣ Recognize the importance of timing, but don't wait for the perfect moment.

♣ Be selective—patience is indeed a virtue.

13

You Can't Get Lucky if You Aren't in the Hand

As much as it's good to be selective about which hands you're going to play, at some point you need to get in the game. If you fold every time, you will never have any shot at winning. Not every hand is going to be a sure thing, but sometimes you get lucky if you just get in there. I personally find that about 30 percent of the hands I win I really shouldn't have but something told me I needed to get in and try.

For example, Melissa was playing in her ten-handed home game, which happened to be comprised of eight men and two women. She was playing by the book and folding her non-premium hands, but every so often, when she could see a flop or a card cheaply, she took the chance and called a small bet. Her 9-7 unsuited in the small blind turned into a straight. It shouldn't have been her win, but she had position, only had to make a small payment, and got lucky.

The same holds true if you are dating. You certainly do not want to go out with everyone who asks you, but at some point you have to pick a few and try. You may not feel like going to fourteen singles parties, but at least if you attend three or four, you have a chance of meeting someone special. What are your odds if you stay home every night? Zero. Luck happens but sometimes; you have to make it that much easier for luck to find you.

You know the old expression "better lucky than smart?" Well, in poker, no matter how good you really are, it helps if you're a little bit lucky. Sometimes, people who really don't know what they're doing will get lucky at your table, but savvy players know that to win consistently, you have to make your own luck. While you may have absolutely no control over the hand you are dealt, you do have control over how you play it. The more you play, the more often you'll see that you're really playing the people, the position, and the situation, more than you are playing the cards in your hand.

Poker is a perfect microcosm for the chaos of life: You never know what you're going to have to tackle next. If you're constantly getting low cards and unsuited cards, not flopping anything, and you just can't get a hand, you may think you're out of luck. But you do have the opportunity, if you're in last position, or if you can identify the person at the table who folds when you raise, to actually do something with a "losing" hand.

You'll find plenty of parallels in business. For example, perhaps you get on a project that you think has no opportunity to become really important. You don't always have the opportunity to change that circumstance, but you can turn it around. You may take a project that no one's really interested in doing and decide you're going to make it more high-profile: find a new hook regarding how it can be done, and *you* make it high-profile and important.

Socially, you can also turn a weak hand into a winner—even if it's not the win you initially envisioned. Let's say you're set up on a blind date, and the minute you see the other person, you absolutely know he's not for you. So you have two choices. You can sit there and you can say, "This person isn't for me, he's not good-looking, he's too short, he has the wrong shoes," and be miserable the whole evening. Or you can say to yourself, "This person isn't for me, but perhaps he's a good business contact, a good date for my friend, or he knows somebody else who would be a better match. Perhaps he'll know somebody who can take care of my dog when I travel."

Away from the Table
Romance and Getting in the Hand

Abby agreed to go out with the brother of her best friend at work when he was visiting from Phoenix. She really didn't want to, but she had spent the last three weekends on the couch eating Froot Loops. She thought there was no chance it would lead to anything because she was firmly planted in Boston, but she went. It turned out they definitely were not a match, but he fixed her up with a sales manager in her region who had just gotten divorced, and the two of them have been dating now for eight months. Now, that's what I call making your own luck!

Luck is an important factor in poker, as it is in everyday life. As a matter of fact, we often overlook the importance of luck because we'd rather focus on certainty. What makes the difference between good poker players and newbies is the attitude they adopt toward luck. All good players admit there is an element of luck to their game and recognize a lucky draw, but do not let it cover for poor play. You won because you were lucky, not because you played a hand particularly well. Also do not be discouraged because of the fact that you experienced an unlucky beat. If you play right, make good decisions, and still lose a hand, stay objective and accept the fact for what it is.

Have you heard about the accuracy of chance? That's luck handed to you on a silver platter. But great things can happen, if you let them. You may not feel like attending another networking event, but if you don't go, you have no chance of meeting a useful contact. Listen to your gut if it tells you to do something. A full and interesting life requires your attendance. You need to show up for yourself to make it all happen.

That's the commonsense aspect of luck, but I'll confess that there's a far more mysterious one. Lucky streaks, for example, make no sense at all but they're real. Sometimes you are in the zone and the gods of luck are with you. You have to be able to recognize and play the streak. There are nights at the card table when you will pick up strong pocket pairs every other hand, or flop the nuts in the big blind with 7-4 off suit. Ride it as hard as you can, because you don't know when it is going to come back. Just make sure when you're "riding the wave" of a lucky streak that you don't get greedy. As soon as you reach your goal—whether it's an amount of money, a great new job, or a wonderful soul mate—don't press your luck. Look what happened to the people who owned trailers at Briny Breezes trailer park just south of Palm Beach, Fla. The location of the trailer park was prime oceanfront property and a developer offered more than $500 million for the land. That means each resident would have gotten about $1 million for a home that in many cases they purchased for less than six figures. But the owners got greedy, and rather than accept the offer and run with their luck, they put the land out for bids from other developers. Well we all know what happened to the real estate market in Florida—and several months later the deal was off. They got greedy and now their hand was dead. They forgot what every poker player knows: Luck will turn. But all the luck in the world isn't going to help you if you stand on the sidelines. You may never know just how lucky you could have been.

Playing Your Game

♣ Test your luck in the right position and you can end up winning a big payout.

♣ Always look for opportunities in what may seem an unlucky situation.

♣ Listen to your gut if it tells you there may be luck to be found.

♣ Ride a lucky streak until you reach your goal, but don't be greedy.

14
The Art of Bluffing

To be a successful poker player, you're going to have to learn how to bluff. The simple reason is that most of the time, you're not going to get good cards. In fact, statistically, you're not going to get good cards about 80 percent of the time. When you're bluffing, you're not playing the cards; you're playing the people, and that's what poker is all about. You don't necessarily have to have the best hand to win; you just have to make people think that you have the best hand. I am often asked, "If bluffing at the poker table is acceptable, is it acceptable to bluff in other areas of your life?" Truth be told, bluffing is a form of deception and no one really wants to deceive, either personally or professionally. But let's face it, everyone tells a little white lie sometimes.

POKERprimaDIVAS® hosted an event one night and, during the instructional phase, we talked about bluffing. One of the participants, a lawyer at a major New York law firm, got upset. Why were we teaching business women—especially attorneys—how to be deceptive? It made us stop and think.

We are not advocating lying, but in order to get ahead you may have to make your boss, competitor, or boyfriend think you have a little more—and in some cases a lot more—than you really do. Basically, we bluff to strengthen our position. The extent of how far you go is up to your own personal ethics. Is it dishonest to tell your on-again, off-again boyfriend that someone else is interested in you in order to push him off the fence? Is it wrong to tell a prospective employer that you have another job offer, even if you don't, to get them to make a quicker decision? Is it wrong to tell a car salesman that you only have $20,000 to spend when you have more? Many people would think of these ploys as perfectly acceptable gamesmanship; others might consider them reprehensible lies. You need to do what you are comfortable with, but, for many, if you want to get ahead in anything, you would be well-advised to brush up on your bluffing skills.

Did you ever meet somebody in business who just seems to glide ahead? They keep getting promoted even though they may not be the sharpest knife in the drawer? They're skillfully diplomatic and have manipulated opinion to make everybody think that they're the best. In a recent *Fast Company* article called "The B in Business Stands for Bluff," the author, Carleen Hawn, quotes poker player Phil Hellmuth: "In what other sport can the player with the least amount of skill, resources, or experience come up a winner, merely on the strength of a bluff? None, except perhaps the sport of business."

And that's what you need to do when you're playing poker. The key to successful bluffing is knowing when to bluff, how to bluff, and whom to bluff. You can't bluff all the time, so you have to choose your timing wisely. Bluffing is a strategy, not a last resort. In poker, a bluff should be a conscientious and calculated decision—not something you do when you're cornered or in a state of desperation.

An important aspect of the bluffing process has to do with knowing whom you are playing. For example, when you're playing or working with people who are fearful, it's easier to bluff than when you're playing with very aggressive opponents who aren't afraid to lose. In a poker game, one of the best times to bluff is when you're in the right position—typically if you're "on the button," i.e., the dealer. This is the position that is last to act and is armed with the most information. The button knows who's bet and who's raised, and of everyone at the table, that person has been able to absorb the most intelligence on which to base the next decision. So when you're last to bet, if you sense weakness at the table and people haven't been betting aggressively, that's an opportunity for you to bluff. Conversely, if everyone is betting and raising, save the bluff for another hand, because you're getting called out. Remember, you're always observing the other players at the table, so you know whom you are playing with. If you've tried to bluff the same person three times and they're calling you, stop bluffing them and pick someone else.

We do this sometimes in relationships. Take Sam and Audrey, who have been together for several years. Sam is a procrastinator and chronically late, which drives Audrey crazy. The bills don't get paid on time. They've missed more than their fair share of airplanes. Audrey bluffs, threatening to break up, and Sam promises to change. He'll get his act together, he says. He just needs another chance. Audrey relents. She'll give him another chance. But Sam thinks she's bluffing and that she doesn't have the nerve to leave, so he keeps going back to his old habits. Truth be told, it's unlikely he ever will change. It's like she's banging her head against the wall. Instead of trying to bluff Sam into changing, Audrey needs to move on to another player. He is who he is. Learn to accept it or cut your losses and move on to the next person.

Remember: If you bluff, sometimes you get called and lose. Don't let that scare you. Just make sure you consider the consequences before you act. If you have never been called on a bluff, chances are you are not taking enough risks. But there are certain guidelines that stack the odds more in your favor. It is easier to bluff one person rather than nine people. If you're at a ten-handed poker table, and everybody is in the hand, you do not want to bluff, because out of a group of nine, somebody's going to call you. You want to bluff when it's just a small group, so that you have less of a chance of being called. The same holds true in a business situation. It is hard to bluff an entire group. (The old saw about being able to "fool some of the people some of the time" comes to mind.)

You also don't want to bluff when the stakes are small enough for an easy call. If there are two or three dollars in play, it isn't much of a risk to call your bluff. That's not the case, however, when there are hundreds or thousands of dollars on the line. Use bluffing as a tool that can put you one step ahead. Don't forget, most of the time, you have to have the goods to win. Bluffing is just the icing on the cake, that extra edge to put you over the top.

The Semi-bluff

Ultimately, in poker, as in life, you cannot bluff every hand. Eventually, someone's going to get better cards and you're going to get caught. That's why timing your bluff is critical. You're typically not going to try to bluff when you're the first one to act, because there are too many people following you that really may have a hand. Try to bluff during a situation where, while you may not have anything right now, you have the potential to have something decent later in the hand. This is known in poker as a semi-bluff.

Semi-bluffs are useful in a business situation, too. On a business interview, you might pretend to have mastered a subject that you actually only partially understand. And that's okay, as long as you can learn it. You may bluff when you're asked to take on an assignment and you're not really 100 percent sure how to complete it, but you know you'll be able to figure it out. Just remember: You have to make sure your bluff is not going to be "called," because if you can't deliver, there will be consequences. Your credibility will take a substantial hit and you might jeopardize a relationship with your boss or friend, so make sure the risk is worth the reward.

The point here is that there's a big difference between bluffing and outright lying. Let's say you have been given an assignment that is due today. You have only completed about 85 percent of the work, but you have a pretty good idea of what the outcome and action plan will be, and could easily talk your way through it and "finish it" in the next day or two. Your boss asks you about the project. Do you bluff your way through, or do you come clean and admit that you haven't completed the assignment on time? Well, that depends on what kind of person your boss is. If you have a boss that is very hands-on and has to know every detail of what you are doing, you will probably have to come clean. However, if you work for a big-picture type who only needs a top-line assessment of all projects and wants only to be reassured that things are getting done, you can probably bluff your way through and get away with it. To bluff effectively, you need to know whom you are dealing with.

If you're on a winning streak, that's a great time to bluff. In a poker game, if you've been winning a lot of hands and have had the opportunity to show your good cards after the final card is turned, then the table starts to think you're on a hot streak. If you then get a lousy hand, but bet it aggressively, everyone will likely think you are still on a hot streak and shy away from playing with you. They may never know you were bluffing.

One of the key things to remember to be successful at bluffing is to know whom you cannot bluff. You don't want to try to bluff someone who has nothing to lose because you will surely be called. And as we've discussed earlier, in a poker game there will be people who just are not going to get out of your way. They are going to call you every single hand because they just want to stay in the action. And those are the people you're never going to try to bluff. This is particularly true when you are a woman at the table.

Away from the Table

Bluffing in a Relationship

Amanda had been dating David for six months on a very regular basis. At age 36, and after numerous mediocre relationships, she thought this was the right guy. However, David had just come out of a dysfunctional relationship and had said several times he wasn't sure he was ready for a stronger commitment. Now Amanda had to make a decision. Was she going to bluff and tell David that she wanted out of the relationship if he would not commit (even though she really wasn't ready to call it quits), or would she just continue with the status quo? Before she could make a decision as to what to do, she had to answer a few questions to see how likely David was to call her bluff and end the relationship. First, she knew David was still very upset about his ex-girlfriend. She was still trying to get back together with him and was, in his words, "stalking" him. Second, David hadn't expressed an interest in having children or even getting married. Last, David had a lot of hobbies and friends—she was hardly his entire world.

Well, Amanda looked at these factors and decided it was not the right time to bluff David. He had too many "outs," and she was not ready to have him call her bluff and end the relationship, so she decided to wait. Amanda was smart. She knew whom she was playing with, looked at his chip stack, and decided to wait for a better bluffing opportunity. Once some time had passed and the ex-girlfriend was no longer a factor and his best friend had moved out of town, she found a better time to make her bluff work for her.

> ## Away from the Table
> ### Bluffing a "Hot Streak" in Business
>
> Sonja was a star in her sales group. She was not only able to get new business into the company, but had a knack for growing sales from her existing client base. For three quarters in a row, she was the top salesperson. During a team meeting with her fourteen colleagues, her boss laid out a list of clients she wanted the group to focus on getting. Sonja wanted two of the clients for herself, as she knew that these were the most lucrative prospects on the list. So she decided to do a little bluffing. After all, she was on a hot streak. She told her boss that she was already working with those two biggest target clients on setting up a deal. No one really questioned her because of her past performance. She did, in fact, know people at these companies, and she was confident that with some hard work, she could get the business. It was a risk, but she was willing to take it, and she was given the go-ahead by her boss to exclusively work to get these companies as new clients. Sonja knew when she was hot and took advantage of it. Her bluff paid off.

Some guys will always call you, as they refuse to be outplayed or bluffed by a woman.

If your bluff isn't working, then you need to know when to stop. Sometimes people begin to bluff and can't walk away from it even when they know that they're beat. Often, you'll see new players bluff a player or two while holding a very poor hand. They get called. Then another card comes down, and they bluff again, only to be called once more. Rather than just cave in and say, "Okay,

I'm beat, these people aren't folding," they continue to throw good money after bad. Sometimes, you have to push your ego to the side, and say, "Okay, I've tried it, I picked the wrong people and I wasn't paying attention, now I've got to get out of my own way." Otherwise, you're going to wind up losing everything—and I'm not just talking about poker chips. Sadly, I've seen people lose their reputations, their relationships, and their jobs from bluffing the wrong people at the wrong time.

Bluffing is an art. It's an art in the game of poker, and it's an art in the game of life. Your objective is to bluff the right people at the right time. And if you can do that, you're going to increase your chances of success at the poker table, in your relationships, and in your business transactions.

Playing Your Game

♣ Don't flat out lie: There's a big difference between lying and bluffing.

♣ Know whom you can and cannot bluff because you may be called.

♣ Choose your time to bluff wisely, taking advantage of perceived weakness.

♣ If you've never been called out on a bluff, you're not taking on enough risk.

15
Sharpening Your Skills

In poker, it's a given that you want to be at a table with weaker players than yourself. Right? Wrong. Obviously, if you want to win a lot of money, it helps to be the strongest player at the table. However, if you want to improve your game, you're going to need to surround yourself with players who are more skillful. There's no better impetus for improvement than keen competition. In fact, when you first sit down in a game, it's best to just sit there and watch so you get an idea of who is a better player.

This also applies to your business life. Certainly, you want to excel and surpass your colleagues, but if you're not working alongside people who can teach you a few tricks, you might find yourself stuck in the ranks. And who wants to be "employee of the month" when you can have a controlling interest in the corporate stock? Once again, it's about setting your sights high enough to justify your efforts. It is also important that you work with people from whom you can learn because that's the only way you're going to get better.

Not the best player at the table? That doesn't mean you should not be playing. Have you ever noticed that certain people will surround themselves with people who are just not as bright as they are in order to feel more secure? You need to surround yourself with smarter, sharper people, too, so you can up your game, both from a poker standpoint and from a professional standpoint. The same holds true in a social setting. You want to have friends that excel in areas where you are weak. Perhaps someone is a financial genius; perhaps they've made a name for themselves in the art world; or perhaps they're confident, responsive parents who seem to be more "on top of things" than most of your peers. While none of them may be perfect, each of your friends should have a quality that you would like for yourself. By surrounding yourself with the people you want to emulate, you'll learn and grow and find new doors opening up to you. As my favorite self-help guru says, "If you are with all your friends and you are the smartest, most successful, most accomplished one of the bunch, you'd better get yourself some more new friends."

Of course, you can also learn something from people who are weak. Good poker players are constantly learning things from lesser players, because they learn what not to do—just like you can learn what not to do by observing certain clueless colleagues. A girl in my office used to chew gum constantly and speak only in a very soft voice. Seeing how unprofessional that looked, I made sure to never do the same. And as great as it is to be in a positive relationship that's moving forward, you can also learn from those situations when things didn't work out if you're willing to emotionally detach and learn from the experience.

Poker players often turn to mentors to improve their game. Professional poker player Evelyn Ng developed her style under the wing of one of poker's top stars, Daniel Negreanu. And when Jamie Gold won the 2006 World Series of Poker Main event, he was conferring with his mentor, another WSOP winner, Johnny Chan, throughout the competition. You don't need to rely only on yourself to learn the skills you need to succeed. When in doubt, seek out a more experienced business colleague, or a girlfriend who can give excellent dating advice, a mother with kids older than yours, or a longtime pet owner who can help with a new dog. If you are willing to keep an open mind and listen to a mentor's advice, you can wind up avoiding a lot of pitfalls.

With or without a mentor by their side, poker players often learn the most by watching past games, both their own and those of other players. Just as in football, the big tournaments are mostly televised, and players record them to examine plays, see what they should have done, and learn from their missteps and triumphs. Analyzing a poker game after the fact, you can see when you should have raised instead of just called, or why you shouldn't have called a certain bet, or why a hand was the wrong one to play.

Though no one is probably filming your daily life, you can still learn a lot from your own actions after the fact in other areas, too. Once a bit of time has passed, you can replay key moments in your head more objectively. Try it and you'll find that the time you spend in quiet reflection can improve your "game."

Away from the Table
Reviewing Your Play for Better Romance

Sara was an intelligent, attractive, funny woman in her 30s everyone seemed to love. No one, including herself, could understand why she was still single. At first, she blamed the guys she dated. They always seemed so great at first, but then as time went by they stopped treating her well. She figured they must have been putting up a front at the beginning to reel her in, when in truth they were just bad guys. But after watching a tape of herself in a poker tournament and recognizing some bad playing habits she had to fix, Sara realized that perhaps she had bad habits in her relationships, too. She "rewound the videotape" on her past couple relationships, thought about her actions, and she figured out that yes, she had been partially to blame for their failure. All along she had easily forgiven her boyfriends for little things—not calling when they said they would, or canceling a date last minute. She thought that made her the "cool girlfriend" who didn't sweat the small stuff. But, in fact, she had been letting these guys know it was okay to treat her inconsiderately. Once she saw her actions objectively, Sara knew she had to stick up for herself more in the future.

Whether you're watching to see how playing certain cards turned out or reexamining events and decisions in your life, an objective eye can let you see what you did wrong—and a smart poker player will always remember her mistakes so as not to repeat them.

Playing Your Game

♣ Find the people from whom you can learn the most.

♣ Keep an eye on weaker company to learn what you should *not* do.

♣ Replay key events after time has passed to figure out what you should not have done and what worked well.

Away from the Table

Rachel had been working in the health and beauty business for about fifteen years and had become very knowledgeable in a lot of different areas. Although very successful, she decided to take a hiatus from what she was doing. A few weeks later, she got a call from a former colleague. Her firm wanted help with a project. Although Rachel specialized in this particular kind of project, she wasn't really interested unless it was profitable enough. In this instance, Rachel knew she was one of the few people with this particular expertise; it was right in her sweet spot. She gave them a price, and they tried to talk her down. She asked for a day to think about it.

Rachel happened to be at a poker game that night, and as she was sitting there, she pulled "pocket aces," the best starting hand you can have. And at that moment, she said to herself, "You know what? I have pocket aces with this assignment! I have the nuts, and if there's any time in my life that I'm going to get what I want, it's now. I have the advantage over everybody else." The next day, Rachel called up her former employers and said, "I'm firm on my price." Sure enough, they came through with it.

They're smart to cash in and take on as many licensing deals as they can while they're still young, healthy, and at the top of their game. There's a limit to how long they can play before they succumb to injury or their fame is eclipsed by the next wave of young talent.

16

Recognize and Exploit Your Strength

When you "have the nuts" in poker, it means you have absolutely the best hand possible. So if you're holding an ace and a king of diamonds, and there are three diamonds on the board, you have the nut flush. Nobody's going to beat you. However, you have to know how to take advantage of the fact that you have the nuts. That means playing your strong hands very aggressively at the right time. The same principle holds true in business.

The interesting thing about poker, though, is that you may have the nuts at the moment but with the turn of a card that may change. With our nut flush example above, if the board pairs on the turn or the river there is the potential for someone to have a full house. Now, all of a sudden, your flush may not the best possible hand and you can no longer be 100% sure will win. It's like these young extraordinary athletes to

So first, you have to know when you have the nuts, and second, you need to know how to play the nuts at the right time.

When you're in a position of strength, it usually means you should be playing very hard and aggressively. Sometimes, however, when you're holding the nuts and it's guaranteed you can't be beat, it is actually better to hold back your betting a little. This way you can draw people in (slow play) to gain more money or whatever it is that you're going after. Let's say you are lucky enough to have started with pocket aces and by the turn you have four aces with no straight flush possible. Now absolutely NOTHING can beat you on the river. You have a sure thing. Some people might think now is a good time to risk all your chips on one hand by going "all-in" but in this case it's not. This is actually a time you would slow play your hand and maybe make what's called a "value bet," a smaller wager that would encourage people to call your bet rather than scaring them away. You're trying to get more money into the pot from the other players. If you went all-in, you might trigger everybody to fold and miss out on accumulating as many chips as you could have possibly solicited. Save your all-in moments for a better time.

When To Go "All-In"

When you're playing no-limit Texas Hold 'Em, at any given moment you are allowed to risk all your chips by going "all-in," risking everything on just one hand. At some point, in order to win a tournament, you're going to need to do this because all-in not only commits you to the pot, but also puts pressure on your opponents and forces them to decide whether or not they're willing to risk going up against you and potentially getting knocked-out or pulverizing their chip stack. You need to look at all the circumstances, your cards, your position, the number of players left, how aggressively everyone is playing, the people whom you're competing with, and the number of chips you've got left. There's always a financial and often an emotional implication for going all-in. You are literally betting all you've got. An all-in move, when timed properly, can produce an enormous payout. Even though you risk a lot when you do it, if you win, you may go from being the short stack to the chip leader.

Many times when you go all-in, you do not want to be called. You are making an aggressive move to win the pot right there and then. You are trying to scare people away so they don't outdraw you or get lucky. Other times you want people to call you so you can win a huge pot, but either way going all-in is a commitment.

Going all-in is revving up your courage and declaring whether or not you're going to fish or cut bait. And we all have to do this too in life, love, business, and yes, poker. If you have strong convictions about something, be it a love interest, a business, an investment, etc., you must be willing to take a stand and make your actions speak very loudly. It's like starting your own company after many years of working for large corporations. You're going all-in, committing your resources, reputation, and usually your own money to this new endeavor.

And what about the notion of going all-in for love? It may be scary and leave you vulnerable but there is no better payout than being connected heart and soul. It may be a gamble, but look at the upside.

If you want to be the winner, at some point you have to make a move. Unfortunately, sometimes we are resistant to this bold strategy when playing poker or making big life decisions. Even when playing for little or no money in a class or low-stakes game, women typically do not go all-in until they're down to their last three or four chips. It is the fear of losing all their chips, and looking stupid or being embarrassed that holds them back.

But when you have fewer chips, you start to lose your edge. And if you become too short-stacked, you can no longer intimidate anybody at the table. If you wait too long, you will whittle down your chip stack, and are going to have to start making desperate moves. You want to go all-in at the right time, but the "right time" is almost never the very last second.

Most male players are constantly pushing their chips into the pot. They'll go all-in on the second or third hand of a tournament, when it really doesn't make sense to do so. Why they do this is one of those head-scratching mysteries. Perhaps it's a testosterone-driven urge. Perhaps men are biologically driven to be more aggressive, and more willing to take risks. Whatever the explanation, women need to get a little bit of this bravado, a little bit of this fearlessness, without losing their own advantage: a tendency to think before acting.

If going all-in doesn't feel right or come naturally, consider this: If it's a disaster, typically, you can start over again. In poker, as in

Away from the Table
Going All-in With Your Career

We had a student recently, Nancy, who was offered a very big job. The only hitch was that job was in Seattle and she was living in Connecticut. Although the job had a great upside, she was agonizing over it. Her friends and family were all on the East Coast. She knew precisely one person in Seattle. She thought it was a huge risk for her. She was happy in her personal life but she was in a rut professionally and felt stuck. She was 32, and wondered what would happen if the job didn't work out for her. What would she do with her life if she moved out there with no fallback plan and no one there to help her pick up the pieces? She was afraid if she failed she would be too embarrassed to come back home.

One night, Nancy came up to me after our fourth lesson and said, "You know, I've been agonizing over this decision, and as we were playing in the tournament and one of my competitors went all-in, it dawned on me: that's what I am contemplating doing with accepting this new job." Something about that moment clicked, and she now had the confidence to make her move. Nancy had gotten into the game of poker because she always wanted to play but thought she wouldn't be good at it. Once she gained some confidence in her skills, she was able to tackle other things in her life that used to intimidate her. Sure enough, she took the assignment in Seattle. We'll wait to see how it turns out. But whatever the result, she took the risk and went all-in and for that reason alone, I'm proud of her.

life, starting from scratch is never the optimal place to be, but it can be done. If you are going to play a high-stakes game, it's important to be comfortable enough to go all-in should that opportunity arise. Sometimes, failure is a necessary option.

So you need to make the commitment with your chips, just like you would need to make a commitment to a job or a spouse or a friend. If it doesn't work out you can build your stack up again.

Playing Your Hand

♣ Recognize when you "have the nuts" and bet that moment, because you may lose out just moments later.

♣ Don't be afraid to ask for more when you have the upper hand.

♣ Hold back when you know you're strong if you sense it will get you more.

♣ Choose a strategic time for your bold risk.

♣ Don't wait until you have too little to risk; you must have enough chips to make your "all-in" worthwhile.

♣ Do not act out of desperation.

♣ Remember that if you fail, you can always start over again.

17
Down Doesn't Mean Out

One of the compelling reasons people play poker is that anybody can be a winner. If you look at the winners of the World Series of Poker for the last seven years, none of them were top players. There's always room for someone to come out of left field and play a better game against the professionals. That's what makes poker so attractive to so many people. If you want to play golf, you're not going to get into a game with Tiger Woods. Or if you want to play basketball, you will most likely not be shooting hoops with LeBron James. But if you have the money to buy into a tournament, you have as much chance of playing with a Daniel Negreanu, Jennifer Harman, or Kathy Liebert as anybody else. Part of the attraction to this game is that the everyday Joe or Joan can gain access to the biggest names in poker. Amateur or pro, anybody can win—even when it looks like you're totally out of luck.

There's actually a very remarkable poker story about a successful player, Jack Straus, who was playing in the World Series of Poker. The game just wasn't going his way, and he silently shoved all his chips in and wound up losing the hand. But when he stood up to leave, he noticed that he had one $500 chip left. Because he had not verbally declared "all-in," he could continue playing. Sure enough, Jack was able to take that one chip and win the 1982 World Series of Poker. Out of that event came what I think is one of the most critical messages of the similarities between life and poker: "All you need is a chip and a chair." Nothing is impossible and there is really nothing in your way except your preconceived notions.

This holds true in any part of your life. The trick to accomplishing most anything is to expand your belief of your own abilities. A man with whom we are all familiar lived his entire life with adversity, but he constantly believed he could achieve. This man:

Failed in business at age 31;

Was defeated in a legislative race at age 32;

Failed again in business at age 34;

Overcome the death of his sweetheart at age 35;

Had a nervous breakdown at age 36;

Lost an election at age 38;

Lost a congressional race at age 43;

Lost a congressional race at age 46;

Lost a congressional race at age 48;

Lost a senatorial race at age 55;

Failed to become vice president at age 56;

Lost a senatorial race at age 58;

Was elected President of the United States at age 60.

With all the adversity he faced, President Abraham Lincoln had no reason to keep trying other than the fact that he believed it was his destiny to succeed. When he seemed down to his very last chip, he used it to win the presidency.

Look at Andy Grove, the former chairman of Intel. Born a Hungarian Jew in 1936, András István Gróf, as he was then known, survived the Nazis only to face the Soviet invasion of his country. He fled to America at age twenty, studied engineering, and arrived in Silicon Valley just in time for a historic opportunity. As talented as he was as an engineer, Grove became an even better manager. This penniless immigrant taught himself to lead a major corporation through some of the toughest challenges in the history of business and became one of the great leaders of American industry.

Or look at the story of Robert Downey Jr., who, after multiple drug arrests, was written off by critics as a Hollywood has-been. But this comeback kid proved the cynics wrong after starring in two box-office runaway successes in 2008, being nominated for an Oscar, and continuing to star in blockbusters.

The great thing about poker is that everybody has an equal opportunity to win. It doesn't matter what school your children attend or what FICA score you have. It doesn't matter what kind of car you drive or what kind of watch you wear. You can be an immigrant from a war-torn country or descended from one of the oldest, most aristocratic families in America. You can be thin or fat, a Ph.D. or a high school dropout. It's a level playing field. We all have the same shot at winning the pot. Your job is to win the most hands you can and make the most money. You just have to adopt the proper mindset.

Talent is important, but practice is critical. People who win poker tournaments, even the lesser-known players who seem to have "come out of nowhere," are typically well-prepared. They play online all day; they read every single book on poker strategy that they can find; they enter as many games as they can. Poker is a big part of their lives. So while they may not be professional, they are well-versed and have done their homework.

As in any pursuit, determination is the key to success. Poker is a game that requires constant learning. Each game is different. The players change, the positions change, the cards change. All of the elements are constantly shifting. It requires patience and tenacity. But if you're ambitious and disciplined, it is a game that you can apply to many facets of your day-to-day existence. While other areas of your life might seem to you to be more restricted, take a good, long look and you will see that in reality, the barriers can be lower than you might imagine. The key is drive, passion, preparation, and a healthy dose of optimism. And, of course, a chip and chair.

Playing Your Game

♣ Remember, you have the same opportunity for success as the person next to you.

♣ Study and prepare to give yourself the best chance to succeed.

♣ Know you can always come back after a "bad beat."

18
The Risk vs. Reward Ratio

A ny player will tell you that poker is a game of skill. In fact, a recent study that analyzed more than 100 million hands of Texas Hold 'Em on Poker Stars (www. pokerstars.com) indicated that more than 75 percent of wins were based on player skill. But many people also like the gambling aspect of poker. If you are a poker player, you are, by definition, a gambler. And being a gambler is nothing to be ashamed of! After all, gambling is nothing more than a calculated risk. Poker players know that in order to improve their chances, they need to understand the risks and rewards of their every action or inaction. Sometimes, failure to act is just as risky as going all-in. In poker, there are certain statistics you need to master to see how likely you are to win.

Poker players learn what is known as "pot odds" to help evaluate the risk vs. reward of being in a hand. You'd be more likely to risk $20 to win a $200 pot, which are 10-to-1 pot odds, than you would to invest $50 to win a $100 pot, which are 2-to-1 pot odds.

Sometimes it pays to take a chance, and sometimes it's just too expensive. The same principles apply when you are looking to get involved in a business deal. You evaluate the financials, see what it is going to cost you, and what the long-term payout is.

Before you bet, you need to understand the probability and payout and ask yourself, given your current hand, is it worth it to stay in? Exactly how much do you stand to gain and how much do you stand to lose? These are not emotional questions but objective statistics. Having the wherewithal to run through these calculations when under pressure will serve you well in all aspects of your life.

You need to make intelligent choices, so you put your time, effort, and money into areas that are going to get you what you want. In the case of a poker game, you're looking to get as many chips as you can. And in your personal life, you're looking to get as much personal fulfillment and happiness as you can get your hands on.

Look at relationships in your life and ask yourself if you are going to have to give too much of yourself in order to get what you want from another person. For instance, getting involved with someone just out of a bad relationship, who maybe has lost a lot of money and is fighting for custody of children, is typically not a great bet. You have to look not just at "the cards in your hand," but also at the surrounding factors to decide if the payout is right for you. You also need to be cognizant of how much risk you are willing to take. Some people have a higher tolerance for risk than others. The most obvious example of risk and reward tolerance relates to investing.

Everyone has a different mindset regarding the stock market. Some invest in shares because of their dividend histories, while others prefer the tried-and-true Blue Chips. Some make their decisions based on the most recent headline and try to amass a position anticipating when a stock will take off. Some play hunches while others create elaborate and detailed spreadsheets. Sometimes it pays and sometimes it doesn't. Everyone always jokes that investing in today's market is like gambling at the casino, but the risk vs. reward calculations and motivations really are similar to playing a game of poker. If you're emotionally attached to your stocks or consumed with guilt about how much you lost in the market last year, chances are you're not going to make logical, rational decisions. Timing is also an important factor in calculating risk vs. reward. If you're about to retire, you're not going to take a very big risk in the stock market, because you're going to need the money in the next few years. Even if it's a sizeable reward, the risk simply isn't worth it. On the other hand, if you have a long investment horizon, you might be more willing to take an aggressive stance—at least with some portion of your portfolio.

Life provides plenty of other examples beyond the financial model. If you're auditioning for a part in a musical and there are one hundred other applicants, you may consider choosing a song and dance routine that is a little daring in order to stand out from the crowd.

In Poker tournaments you're going to take on a lot less risk at the beginning of the tournament, simply because you don't want to get knocked out quickly, and usually the reward isn't as big, since people have not amassed very large chip stacks yet. However, later on in the tournament, when you're down to fewer players and each player has a greater stack that you can win, you're going to start taking on more risk, because you need to start accumulating ever larger amounts of chips if you want to get into first place. For example, on the first day of a tournament, you may actually consider folding pocket kings pre-flop following a raise and a re-raise. Under most circumstances, you wouldn't do that later in a tournament.

Discipline is also critical in a poker game and can greatly influence your probability and payout. We know how foolish it can be to get involved in every hand or every business deal or too many relationships because when the "good one" comes along, chances are you'll be short of resources. So the key is having the discipline to wait for a good opportunity so you can maximize your payout. As my good friend Bill, an investment consultant, says, "If you buy a stock and it doubles, no matter how great the prospects are, take some money off the table. Sometimes the bulls win, sometimes the bears win, but the pigs never win."

I see this all the time at the poker table. A player amasses four or five times their initial chip stack and then starts to hit a losing streak that eats away most of the winnings. Some people think they can win forever, and some people are simply afraid to walk away a loser. Rather than walking away with a portion of his winnings, this player keeps trying to win it back. And the harder he tries, the more he loses, until he loses his entire stack. You see stock market investors doing this as well; they don't want to admit failure. Having already lost money, they are afraid to lose pride, too. Thus, rather than cutting their losses and moving on to other investments, people will often stubbornly hold onto their unsuccessful investments. People hate to admit they were wrong. It becomes emotional rather than about the numbers. And when you get emotional, all logic goes out the window.

Even romantic relationships are subject to risk/reward calculations. What are you willing to risk? Are you going to get involved emotionally with a person who travels 90 percent of the time, or never keeps a job, or has a history of dating multiple women simultaneously? Is it worth putting your emotions on the table when you consider the likely outcome? Probably not. If you're with somebody with a history of long-term relationships who's loving and caring, you'll be more comfortable making an emotional commitment, because your chances of having a good relationship are much better. I think women in relationships have to be careful what they put out there. We often put more at risk than we can get back in reward.

Most people think that women are risk-averse, but a survey of more than 650 women managers polled during the 2008 Simmons School of Management national leadership conference revealed that businesswomen are highly likely to take risks related to business or professional opportunities. When women were asked about business/professional opportunities taken, such as new jobs,

Away from the Table:
Taking a Risk with Your Career

K atie worked for a publishing company in New York and had been on her job four years. Her boss was a total slacker and, Katie, being a dedicated worker, had been doing her boss's job along with her own for longer than she cared to admit. Her boss took all the credit for anything good that came out of the department, but put the blame on Katie if something went wrong. Katie was just miserable. She knew she had to do something or she would never be promoted and continue to be frustrated in her career. She had mentioned the problem to her supervisor several times to no avail. Her only option was going to her boss's boss. In doing so, she knew the risk was not only alienating her boss but also the higher-ups, as typically supervisors do not like it when a junior person goes above their superior's head. However Katie also saw the silver lining. Her reward was that she would be more satisfied at work and maybe even get promoted. It was a tough decision, but Katie decided to go to the higher-ups and tell them the situation. Unfortunately, they sided with her boss. Katie was very upset. She spent the next three months walking on eggshells at work and looking for a job in her free time. She eventually left and wound up getting a great job with a better title at another publishing house. Katie took a risk and, at the outset, it looked like the risk did not payoff. But six months later, Katie had a much better job and salary, fantastic co-workers, and was much happier. And to top it off, her boss that she had complained about failed miserably after she left and wound up getting fired, which felt like vindication for Katie.

assignments, programs, or change initiatives, all of which involved the investment of personal capital and carried unknown outcomes for both the business and for personal/career development:

80 percent reported pursuing a major change initiative "sometimes" or "often";

79 percent reported pursuing a new program;

77 percent reported pursuing a new job;

56 percent reported pursuing a major business development opportunity.

Poker offers a great opportunity to increase your risk profile in all areas of life. Going for it, taking a risk—even if it doesn't immediately seem to work out—is sometimes still better than doing nothing.

I find that we seldom regret what we do. Instead, we regret what we didn't do. As Rear Admiral Grace Murray Hopper is reported to have said, "It's easier to ask forgiveness than it is to get permission."

Playing Your Hand

♣ Evaluate your risks and rewards before you act so you can bet small and win big.

♣ Save your emotional and financial resources for the right opportunity and don't whittle down your stack because you jumped into too many of the wrong things.

♣ Calculate "pot odds" to determine how much you can gain compared to your investment.

♣ Consider timing when taking a risk; where you are in life determines how much you have to lose.

19
Stay On Your Game

Sometimes you do everything right and still lose. There are nights you're at the poker table and feel like your game is dead-on. You're playing your cards the right way and you're doing everything right, but you're still losing. Just to rub it in, there'll be other players who do everything wrong and still win. I don't know if it's bad luck, bad karma, or just your environment, but you will sometimes play perfectly and lose. The best you can do is to not let it discourage you from going on to the next hand.

Failure to shake off a "bad beat" (or even a series of them) can lead to a phenomenon called "going on tilt." In poker, this means letting your game go off-track because you're so upset over what happened, you're so angry, that you're just not playing your game right. It's "losing your focus" writ large. In poker, as in life, when your emotions take control, your game is in serious jeopardy.

We frequently go on tilt in our everyday lives as well. Ever return a terrific dress out of spite because the store manager refused to adjust your receipt to reflect a subsequent price reduction? What about firing off a nasty e-mail to a colleague because you thought a previous one was insulting or dismissive? Yell at a reckless taxi driver for taking the wrong route and wind up letting it ruin your dinner? Well if you have, you know what it is like to be on tilt. And you also know that if you had just taken a deep breath, let a bit of time pass (even just counted to ten), and thought about your actions before you reacted emotionally, you'd be better off for it.

Away from the Table
Going on Tilt Socially

Karla and Alexa went to UCLA together and were in a sorority with several other women who now lived in the Chicago area. One night they were out for dinner and saw their good friend Wendy's husband out with another woman. The two were drinking wine seated on a double banquet and holding hands. Karla couldn't believe it. Enraged, she said to Alexa, "I am going to pour a drink over his head and then call Wendy and tell her what we saw!" But Alexa stopped Karla in her tracks.

"Some women might not want to know their significant other is cheating," Alexa reasoned, "and I think Wendy is one of them." Alexa had once seen a movie with Wendy about a cheating husband. At the time, Wendy told her that if she were in a similar circumstance, she would not want to know. Had Karla gone on tilt and carried out her threatened confrontation with Wendy's cheating husband, she would have done more harm than good. Whether she agreed with Wendy's philosophy on the matter was irrelevant. She almost let her emotions overtake her reason.

A bad beat in poker happens when you play strong cards in the right way, so you're statistically favored to win, but because of a lucky draw, someone else with a weaker starting hand still beats you. There's nothing you could have done to prevent it. Like in horse racing, sometimes a specific horse can be the odds-on favorite with the best record, and so you bet on it. But at the very end of the race another horse—ranked toward the bottom, like Mine That Bird in the 2009 Kentucky Derby—finds the sudden strength to win. You played the odds right, but you never could have known that lucky horse would come from behind.

And a bad beat can also happen to you in a relationship. Sometimes you meet somebody, and you take the right amount of time to get to know each other, you put enough pressure on them to move the relationship forward, you spend the right amount of time together, but unfortunately, you're involved with somebody who's just not ready to get serious. Or perhaps fate intervenes and one of you has to move for a job, or a family member gets sick and priorities shift. You did everything right, but it didn't work out.

Jobs and business projects are also subject to the "no-fault failure" phenomenon. Did you ever work on a project in which you had the right team, sufficient time, and even an adequate budget, but still couldn't make it work? Trust me, if you haven't had this experience yet, you will. And when it does happen to you, you can either waste your time parsing the experience for mistakes that either didn't happen or couldn't have been prevented, or you can pick yourself up and try again. You can't let a bad beat ruin your entire game.

Away from the Table
Coping With a Career Setback

Jane was called for a job interview at a vitamin company in Phoenix. They found her through a headhunter and she was selected from more than fifty people based on her résumé and a phone interview. They flew her to Phoenix to meet the key company executives. Jane spent an entire day with the team and she thought she aced the interview. She clicked with everybody, and it turned out that she knew one of the executives from her previous job and he was really crazy about her work.

When the interview concluded, the human resource person said, "We're interviewing six people, and we are going to have three of them back." Jane was sure that she would be one of the three. But she got an e-mail a few days later saying that she was not one of the candidates selected to come back. Jane was devastated! She just couldn't understand what went wrong. Then about six months later, she learned that the company's new hire was brought over from Europe. It was somebody that they had promised would be brought to the U.S., and this was the only job that they could find for him. In other words, no matter how well-qualified she was, she wasn't getting the job. She did everything right, but for reasons she couldn't control, the job was never going to be hers.

But she didn't let her disappointment stop her. She wrote a note to the president saying that she hoped things were going well. It was a gracious letter without a hint of bitterness and it served her well. She didn't wind up with a job from that company, but she did wind up getting connected to another great opportunity. She didn't "go on tilt"; instead, she wound up winning.

The other key to coping with a bad beat is to avoid pursuing revenge. Jane could have easily written to the executive recruiter and said she felt misled and would never work with him again. Or she might have written to the president of that company saying that he had treated her unfairly. But where would either of these actions have left her? If Jane had gone on tilt looking for revenge, she'd never have gotten the career opportunity that came her way later. Always consider that when you let your negative emotions take over, you usually wind up losing the hand.

During the World Series of Poker 2008 games, there was a situation when one player had pocket aces, and the other had two suited cards. What wound up happening is that the person with the pocket aces got four aces, but on the river, the person with the two suited cards beat those four aces with a royal flush. The odds of that happening are incalculably small, and that is truly a bad beat that could have caused the opponent to go on tilt. He didn't. He continued to play and kept his focus on the next hand. He remembered a critical poker rule: There's always another hand.

Although it's not a rule, it's generally wise to keep quiet about your bad beats. If you're having a fight with your spouse or a standoff with your boss, everybody doesn't need to know about it. You can confide in a few of your closest friends, but there are perils to sharing too much information about any aspect of your life. One risk is that by dwelling on the negative, you'll alienate lovers, colleagues, and friends—precisely the people who can help when life takes a downward turn. Nobody wants to be around a perpetually negative

Away from the Table
Going on Tilt Romantically

Ruthie came to class one night in a total tizzy. Her boyfriend had been working on a movie deal like a maniac for five weeks and had been very unavailable. He was sleeping four hours a night and was living on soda, coffee, and Doritos. He had sent her a text in the morning that he might be able to see her for a few hours that evening and would get back to her later in the day. By 7 p.m., she still had not heard from him, and she was so steamed she could hardly see straight. How could he be so thoughtless, how could he ignore her? She was done. She could not take it anymore. When he finally did call, she went off on him. He was stunned and angry. He felt wronged since he was the one working like a dog. Needless to say, they did not see each other that night.

Still reeling, Ruthie called one of her most successful guy friends and told him the story. She didn't get the response she anticipated. Her friend condemned Ruthie for going off on her boyfriend. Her boyfriend needed support, and if he could not get it from her, she certainly was not going to get what she wanted. She thought about it and blurted out to the group, "I went on tilt. I couldn't just go on to the next hand and see what happened."

The next time Ruthie's boyfriend called, he said he couldn't meet her until the deal was done. She was still steaming mad, but instead of screaming at him and being overrun by her emotions, she sent him over a pint of ice cream to show her support. He really appreciated the thought, and he made it up to her as soon as his deal was finished.

person. So if you can learn something from the bad beat in poker, it's that it's better to keep a lid on it and wait for your next hand.

Everyone has a bad beat story—and poker players have more than most. You are not alone. So if you have a bad beat, the key is to get past it. Know that there's always another hand. And whatever you do, don't let it influence your next round of play.

The other thing you need to avoid doing is trying to get even. In poker games, some players get so upset about losing money that they will go on a mission to win back what they lost. They may start playing every hand or go to a higher stakes table. Their mindset is such that they do desperate things and usually wind up losing more because of it. In relationships, you might compare it to trying to get revenge. You may get so thrown off by rejection or hurt that you want nothing more than to get back at the other person. Passed over for a promotion? Now it's time to get back at your boss. But really, what does that get you in the end? Don't try to get even. It's time-consuming and exhausting.

I like Suzy Welsh's concept of "10-10-10," thinking about the importance of considering how an action will affect you in 10 minutes, 10 months, and 10 years. Indulging an urge to strike back might make you may feel better for a few minutes or win you back a little money, but beyond the initial satisfaction, typically you will feel worse. It just saps your energy and you risk losing more time, money, and face.

Playing Your Game

♣ Keep your cool if you do everything right and still lose. There's always another hand.

♣ Don't go on tilt. Accept that a situation isn't fair rather than letting it rattle you and sway your focus.

♣ Avoid making your bad beat stories too public.

♣ Don't let your emotions lead you to make desperate actions.

♣ Don't try to get even.

20

Men vs. Women: The Double Standard

More books have been written on male-female relationships, tendencies, and behavior than almost any other topic. I'm certainly not going to try and explain the complexities of these gender differences here. We all know that women have always coped with a double standard when it comes to being judged for the same actions, qualities, or achievements as men. It's easy to dismiss this fact as cliché, or to brush it off with a wave of the hand. Legally, a woman can hold almost any job a man can, she can hold the same advanced degrees; no one is surprised if she can support herself on her own. But men and women are different. They tend to go about their life and their business differently—and get judged by different standards. You need go no further than the poker table to see this all in action.

As the president and founder of POKERprimaDIVAS®, I am frequently asked, "Is there an advantage to being a female at the poker table?" Actually, there are many. Women typically have a much keener intuition than men and are also better at paying attention to detail. We're good at picking up tells and we're especially good at reading men, because that's what we've been doing since we started dating. We're constantly evaluating every word and action, parsing them for clues. Finally, we're typically just a little more patient. We're willing to sit out more hands in order to observe and wait until we have a good hand. These are strong skills to bring to the poker table!

These same abilities are valuable to us in the workplace. There is nothing wrong with using your femininity, or the traits that you have as a woman, to get what you want out of a poker game, a business deal, or life in general. The key to winning a "man's game," therefore, is not to become a man, but to leverage all the advantages you have as a woman.

In the poker world, men and women are said to play differently. As with any stereotype, sometimes this is true and sometimes not. Typically, the "male" style of play is to be aggressive, to raise often, and to play a less-than-ideal hand knowing you can pressure another player into folding. Women are supposed to be more patient and less aggressive. Perhaps they fold more hands, waiting for better cards to play, and a better chance to win. Perhaps their raises are smaller, their risks less extreme. Some women will want to "play like a man," to push an opponent, to be aggressive. And when a woman engages this strategy? More often than not, she's labeled as "bitchy"—while if a man plays the same way, with the same actions and bravado, then he is congratulated.

Look at what happened at the 2008 World Series of Poker Main Event. Tiffany Michelle was the only woman to make the top 20, and the media focused on her intensely. Michelle played aggressively, even with attitude, as many men have before her. At one point, she called "the clock" on a player with a big hand who had been taking way too long, giving the player just one minute to make a decision about his cards. Although she was not one of the players in the hand, she was well within her rights—and following the written rules—to ask for a time limit to keep the game moving, which can be crucial in tournament play. The backlash she received was extreme. The men at the table, and later the poker media and online forums, tore her apart for what they called a horrible breach of poker etiquette. In fact, if you watch her on TV, she does come off as being somewhat obnoxious and antagonistic. However, we know they edit the footage to enhance the drama—it makes for better TV. In several online interviews she explained that the rapidly escalating blinds caused her to call the clock to protect her chip stack.

Now fast-forward to several months later, to the World Series of Poker Europe, where a male player, Bengt Sonnert, faced a nearly identical situation. With about 20 players left in the competition, he called "clock" on an important hand that was taking too long. This time however, no one at the table, in the media, anywhere, made a peep of protest. I guess men are expected to behave this way, but women are not.

You see a lot of the "playing like a man" and "playing like a woman" in politics. When Hillary Rodham Clinton became the first woman to put in a serious bid for the presidency, she often seemed at pains to de-emphasize that fact. At times, she went on the offensive against her opponent, turning on the aggression. We need a strong president, no one would deny that. However, Clinton seemed to be fighting her more feminine traits, her vulnerability, her heart, and her appearance, which could have worked to her advantage. And so even though she possessed the intelligence necessary for the position, the end result was that she came across to many as unlikable. Sarah Palin, on the other hand, absolutely relied on her feminine wiles on the campaign trail. She portrayed herself as a mother, a best friend, and even sometimes a bookish sex symbol. And, in fact, a certain segment of the public loved her persona—that is, until she began to appear less and less intelligent. But what might have happened had Clinton let herself come across in a similar way as Palin—as vulnerable, motherly, and feminine—while having the chops to back it up? A woman need not always play like a man to get ahead. She has her own chips, and if she plays them in her own style but with skill and strategy, her chances of success are very high. Men in politics have it easier— they can appear unintelligent and still become president! They can lapse morally or sexually and still remain president! A woman, however, needs to have it all.

So then what do you, as a PokerWoman™, do about the double standard? First, accept that it exists. It's there, it's unfair, but you can thicken up your skin and make it work for you. It isn't unfeminine to play the game on your own terms, and you shouldn't change your style because someone else might critique it. When

Michelle was asked if she would call "clock" again in a similar situation, she said she absolutely would. She wanted to win and she was going after what she wanted. You can't let criticism throw you off your game.

You'll see a lot of recklessness with men that you typically see less of in women. Learn to identify it and use it to your advantage. Once when I was at a poker table, a typical bully player had been trying to intimidate me. He played every hand no matter how weak it was, and he raised often, especially against me. So when I started out with ace, king, I kept raising as the hand went on, and he kept calling. But my intuition and his past style of play told me I had a better nothing hand. Then, on my last raise, he re-raised me for all his chips. I had nothing but ace high, but I had sized him up, I had read him, and I called. I won. Immediately he blew up, ranting about how stupid it was to call with my hand, and no one who knew anything would have called him. But if we had been in the opposite situation, he would have gone on about how brilliant he'd been to have the guts to make the call.

When someone's over-aggressiveness gives you an opportunity, don't be afraid to take what you can. Guys have no trouble asking for and going after what they want. Women are told not to offend, not to be "bitchy." But no criticism should stop you from going after what you want.

Playing Your Game

♣ Don't be afraid to "play like a man" and go after what you want—it doesn't mean you are bitchy!

♣ Thicken up your skin and don't let criticism throw you off your game.

♣ Leverage the innate advantages of your feminine wiles to play your best game possible.

♣ Act on someone's masculine aggression if it offers you an opportunity to get what you want.

21
Stack the Deck in Your Favor

Everyone comes to the table with her own chips. Some might start with more than another, but in poker, as in life, if you play your chips correctly, you can start to build up your stack. The chips don't stay in one place for long, and you can win them if you know how. So what stack are you starting with? You may possess looks, money, personality, intelligence, sophistication, wit, kindness, a great job, education, contacts, cars, houses, a spouse, kids, organizational skills, a great figure, athleticism, or whatever else you might bring to the table. And if you use what you have, you can get the life you want. If you are lacking chips in one area, then use the ones you have to get what's missing. A woman in need of a job uses her intelligence, education, and contacts to find a new position. A single person will use her looks, personality, and wit to find a new love. The key is to recognize what chips you have, know the ones you want, and start betting on yourself.

Away from the Table
Betting on Yourself

Our friend Jessica had a knack for making friends. Though she wasn't the most physically attractive woman in the room, and her college degree wasn't from any particularly impressive school, she had a sunny disposition, a sense of humor, and a warm personality that drew people to her. When Jessica—like many in her pharmaceutical company—got laid off last winter, she took stock of her situation. She hadn't loved her job. Jessica wasn't a natural go-getter. Perhaps because of low self-esteem, or a reluctance to ask for people's help, she had never before thought of changing her career.

But Jessica had a Facebook network of hundreds of friends and contacts, all of whom loved her and wanted to help her. Within days of sending out the word on Facebook, Jessica had multiple interviews set up, and she wound up finding a new career in the public relations industry that she liked much better than her old one. By using her moderate chip stack in the most strategic way, Jessica wound up winning the pot she wanted.

The chips you bring to the table also contribute to your image, and your image plays a huge role in poker, in business, and in relationships. Someone with an Ivy League MBA, who dresses like a Brooks Brothers mannequin and drives a BMW, will have a very different image than an F.I.T. graduate who wears vintage clothing and hops around town by subway. And, like it or not, people are going to treat you differently based on your chip stack and image. Sometimes that will work for you, and sometimes it won't. Our Ivy Leaguer might have a tougher time getting a job at a roll-up-your-sleeves young start-up company, but an easier time getting into a Hamptons golf club. The thing about image, though, is that you can manipulate it in order to make it work for you.

When Jessica talks about how she adjusts her image at the poker table, she has different strategies with men than with women. When playing against men, she tends to dumb it down and—if she's being honest—sometimes sex it up. Her competition thinks she has no idea what she's doing, or they'll be too distracted to care. But at a women-only tournament, she knows it's her intelligence that will keep the other players guessing. By projecting a savvier image, she's more likely to scare others out of a pot.

When it comes to relationships, Sara doesn't shy away from using similar tactics. An attractive woman with a nice figure, she doesn't consider it beneath her to flirt with a man in order to get what she wants. If she charms a mâitre d', for instance, she gets a better table. By portraying the more traditional feminine image of being pleasant and alluring, she's more likely to win a pot at an all-male table. But around women, she relies solely on her intelligence. By portraying herself as an authority figure, by impressing with her cleverness, she can go all-in and come out with the winning hand. Whether what she does is "admirable" is up for interpretation. But Sara knows what she has, knows how to use it in the most effective way, and does so in order to get what she wants. She is focused and aggressive. And that doesn't mean she is nasty or unfeminine, that she doesn't cry or have a bad day. She can be warm and friendly and kind.

If you watched Donald Trump's *Celebrity Apprentice* in 2009, you know that Annie Duke, one of the world's greatest poker players, was one of the final two contestants, competing against Joan Rivers for the ultimate win. Annie did better than Joan on the tasks. She was smart, tough, and strategic. But she failed in one area. She was not as well-liked and she alienated many of the people whose support she ultimately needed to win. Had she portrayed a more gracious image and remained a little more people-focused rather than task-focused, she might have won.

The best thing about poker, and in many ways the best thing about life, is that anyone can win or lose at any given moment. Who holds the short stack and who reigns as chip leader can change at the drop of a dime. No matter what you bring to the table, if you play intelligently, you always have the possibility of winding up the winner. Poker is an equal opportunity game. What's more, everyone has a bad beat story—it's not just you. When you play the game, even if you play it as well as you can, sometimes you're going to lose. But the same goes for the person next to you, and the person next to her. The saying "all you need is a chip and a chair" resonates with players each and every day. When you're down to your very last chip, if you're still willing to play it, you can be back in the game on the very next hand. Your situation is never as bad as it seems.

When faced with a bad beat, the PokerWoman™ gets back on her feet, doesn't let it faze her for long, and focuses her skill and energy on the next hand in front of her. Your situation can change in an instant. Just look at Susan Boyle, a seemingly unremarkable contestant on *Britain's Got Talent,* a televised variety show contest. She had one chip—her singing—and she waited for the perfect opportunity to play it. After just one televised singing performance, which then became a YouTube sensation, she turned into a world-famous star. Now that is a PokerWoman™, taking a stack and turning it into an enormous pile of chips.

Everything can change in an instant. Your cards will change, your luck will change, your streak will change, and everyone is susceptible. If you are a PokerWoman™, then you'll know how to stay in the game and forget an unfair past in order to concentrate on playing in the present to improve your future. Figure out the kind of game you want to play, the goals you want to achieve, the image you want to project, and the life you want to live. If you stick to your game plan in the long term, you have every chance of being successful and happy. A PokerWoman™ knows what she wants and goes for it. See you at the table.

Playing Your Game

- ♣ Use the chips you *have* to get the ones you *want*.
- ♣ Manipulate your image to make a situation work best for you.
- ♣ Always get back on your feet after a bad beat.
- ♣ Know your game plan.
- ♣ Fearlessly go after the win to get what you want.

Appendix

Below are the hands of poker, ranked in order from highest to lowest.

Royal Flush

The five highest cards, the 10 through the ace, all five of the same suit. A royal flush is actually an ace-high straight flush.

Straight Flush

Any five cards of the same suit in consecutive order. Ace can be high or low.

Four of a Kind (aka Quads)

Four cards of the same denomination.

Full House (aka "A boat")

Any three cards of the same value, plus any pair of a different value. Ties are broken first by the three of a kind, then the pair.

Flush

Any five non-consecutive cards of the **same suit**. This example shows a queen high diamond flush.

Straight

Any five consecutive cards of mixed suits. Ace can be high or low. This example shows a six-to-ten straight.

Three of a Kind (aka Trips or a Set)

Three cards of the same denomination.

Two Pair

Any two cards of the same value, plus any other two cards of the same value. If both hands have the same high pair, the second pair wins. If both pair tie, high card (Kicker) wins.

Pair

Any two cards of the same denomination.

High Card-Nothing Hand

No two cards have the same rank, are not in order, and are not all of the same suit. This is an ace high hand.

How to Play Texas Hold 'Em

The objective is to make the best five-card hand combining your "hole cards" and the five community cards face-up on the board.

Someone is designated the dealer. That person is handed the "button."

The player two seats to the left of the button is the "big blind." That person has an automatic, predetermined, forced bet before the cards are dealt. The blind amounts are determined in advance of play.

The player immediately to the left of the button is the "small blind." That person is forced to put up half the bet of the big blind before the cards are dealt.

Everybody is dealt two cards face-down, starting with the small blind. These are called hole cards. Do not let anyone see them. Protect your hand. Everyone looks at their cards and then the first round of betting occurs with the person to the left of the big blind (This is called "under the gun.")

To stay in the hand you must "call" or match the big blind or, if someone has raised, match their bet or raise it. If you do not wish to bet, raise, or call, you fold.

Once the betting stops, the "flop," or, the first three cards, are dealt. These are community cards and everybody can use them.

There is another round of betting that begins with the person to the immediate left of the button.

You may check (pass) if no one has bet, call a bet, raise the bet, or fold.

The next card (aka fourth street, the TURN) is now dealt face-up.

There is another round of betting.

The next card is dealt face-up, fifth street (the river).

There is a final round of betting.

The players left in the hand turn-up their cards and the best five-card hand wins the pot. You can use three or four of the community cards in combination with your hand, or sometimes you will just play the five community cards on the board.

NOTE—In no-limit games, you can bet as many chips as you have in front of you.

Slang Names for Poker Hands

A-A: **American Airlines, Pocket Rockets**

K-K: **Cowboys**

Q-Q: **Ladies, Siegfried and Roy**

J-J: **Hooks**

A-J: **Blackjack**

A-K: **Big Slick, Anna Kournikova (looks good, never wins)**

K-J: **Kojak**

J-4:   **Flat Tire ("What's a jack for?")**

J-5:   **Jackson 5**

A-8:   **Dead Man's Hand**

9-8:   **Oldsmobile**

8-8:   **Snowmen/Two Fat Ladies**

4-5:   **Jesse James**

3-A: **Baskin-Robbins**

3-8:   **Raquel Welch**

A-10:   **Johnny Moss**

10-2:   **Doyle Brunson**

2-9:   **Twiggy**

5-10:   **Woolworth**

5-5:   **Speed Limit**

Glossary

Aces Full

A full house with three aces and any pair.

Aces Up

Two pairs, one of which is aces.

Action

The amount of betting activity during a hand. Multiple bets and raises is a lot of action.

All-in

When all your chips are in the pot. In table stakes games, a player may not go into his or her pocket for more money during a hand. If the player runs out, a side pot is created in which that player has no interest. However, he or she can still win the pot for which he had the chips.

American Airlines
Term used for a pair of aces. (See Pocket Rockets.)

Ante
Amount of money or chips each player puts in the pot before the cards are dealt. Most hold 'em games do not have an ante; they use blinds to get initial money into the pot.

Backdoor Straight
When the last two cards make a player's hand, even though he or she played on the flop for some other reason.

Backdoor
Catching both the turn and river card to make a drawing hand.

Bankroll
The amount of money you have available to wager.

Belly Buster
A draw to fill an inside straight.

Bicycle/Wheel
A straight that is A-2-3-4-5. Usually the best low hand in a high/low game.

Big Blind
The forced bet in second position before any cards are dealt.

Big Slick

A hand that contains an A-K.

Big Stack

The person or people at the table with the largest amount of chips.

Blind

A forced bet (or partial bet) put in by one or more players before any cards are dealt. Players immediately to the left of the button put in blinds.

Bluff

Pretending to have better cards than you actually do. A player who bluffs usually bets higher than his/her cards warrant. The desire of the bluffer is to scare the other players out of the hand by making them think he/she is holding outstanding cards.

Board

The face-up cards or community cards on the table.

Boat

Another term for a full house.

Bottom Pair

A pair with the lowest card on the flop. If you have K♦-5♣, and the flop comes J♣-8♦-5♣, you have flopped bottom pair. (5s.)

Broadway

An ace-high straight (A-K-Q-J-10).

Bullet

Another term for an ace.

Burn

To discard the top card from the deck, face down. This is done between each betting round before putting out the next community card(s). It is security against any player recognizing or glimpsing the next card to be used on the board.

Button

A white disk used to indicate who the dealer is. Also used to refer to the player on the button. Example: "Oh, the button raised."

Buy-in

The minimum amount of money required by a player to sit down in a particular poker game.

Cap

In limit games, the limit on the number of raises in a round of betting.

Cash In

To leave the game and convert one's chips to cash, either with the dealer or at the cage.

Cash Out

To leave a game and cash in one's chips.

Chase

To stay in against an apparently stronger hand, usually in the hope of filling a straight or flush.

Check

To not bet, with the option to call or raise later in the betting round. Pass.

Check Raise

To check and then raise when a player after you bets.

Chop

To return the blinds to the players who posted them and move on to the next hand if no other players call. It also means to "split the pot."

Collusion

When two or more players conspire to cheat in a poker game.

Come Over the Top

To raise or re-raise an opponent's bet.

Community Cards

These are cards that are dealt to the table. All players can use these cards to complete a five-card hand.

Connector
A hold 'em starting hand in which the two cards are one apart in rank. Examples: Q-J, 3-4.

Cowboy
Another term for a king.

Dead Money
Money put into the pot by players who have already folded.

Drawing Dead
Drawing in a situation where even if the draw is made, the hand is still a losing hand. Example, you could be playing a flush draw, but if your opponent has a full house, you'd be drawing dead.

Drawing Hand
A hand that will not win unless it is improved on the draw.

Ducks
A pair of twos (deuces).

Early Position
The players who will act first when the betting starts. Usually the first three positions.

Fifth Street
The fifth and last community card on the board, otherwise known as "the river."

Flop

The first three community cards, put out face-up, all together.

Fold

This is when players throw in their cards. They give up any claim on the pot in exchange for not having to contribute more money to the pot.

Fourth Street (otherwise known as "the Turn")

The fourth community card that is dealt after the flop.

Free Card

Seeing fourth or fifth street without having to place a bet. This happens when everyone checks rather than bets.

Heads-up

When only two players are left in a hand.

Hole Cards

These are the down cards in front of the players.

Inside Straight

Four cards that require another between the top and the bottom card to complete a straight. Players who catch this card make an inside straight. For example: 6, 7, 8, 10 (need a 9).

Kicker

An unpaired card used to determine the better of two near-equivalent hands. For instance, suppose you have A-J and your opponent has A-9. If the flop has an ace in it, you both have a pair of aces, but you have a jack kicker. Also used as a tiebreaker.

Ladies

A pair of queens.

Late Position

The players who act toward the end of the round of betting. In a nine-handed game, the seventh, eighth, and ninth players to act are in late position.

Middle Position

The players who act in the middle of the betting round. If there are nine players, middle position players are the fourth, fifth, and sixth to act.

Minimum Buy-in

The least amount of money with which you can start a game.

Monster

A very big hand.

Move In

To go all-in.

Muck

The pile of folded and burned cards in front of the dealer, or to discard or fold a hand.

No-limit

A version of poker in which a player may bet any amount of chips (up to the number in front of them) whenever it is his or her turn to act.

Nuts

The best possible hand given the board. If the board is K♠-J♦-T♠-4♠-6♥, then A♠-Q♠ is the nuts. You will occasionally hear the term applied to the best possible hand of a certain category, such as nut flush or nut straight.

Offsuit

A hold 'em starting hand in which the two cards are of different suits.

Open

To make the first bet.

Open Ended Straight

Four consecutive cards whereby one additional (consecutive) card is needed at either end to make a straight. 4, 5, 6, 7 can win with an 8 or a 3.

Out

A card that will make your hand win. Normally heard in the plural. Example: "Any spade will make my flush, so I have nine outs."

Overcard

A card higher than any card on the board. For instance, if you have A-Q and the flop comes J-9-6, you don't have a pair, but you have two overcards.

Pocket Cards

The face down cards dealt to each player at the start of each hand. Also called Hole Cards.

Pocket Pair

A pair in a player's face down cards, such as 10♦-10♥.

Pocket Rockets

A pair of aces dealt as hole cards.

Position

A player's turn to act in respect to others at the table. Position is a key factor in almost any fixed-position game like Texas Hold 'Em.

Rainbow

A flop that contains three different suits, thus no flush can be made on the turn. Can also mean a complete five-card board that has no more than two of any suit, thus no flush is possible.

Raise

Not only matching, but increasing the bet amount made by another player.

Rake

An amount of money taken out of every pot by the dealer—this is the cardroom's income.

River Card

The fifth and final community card, put out face up, by itself. Also known as fifth street.

Second Pair

A pair with the second highest card on the flop. If you have A♠-T♠, and the flop comes K♦-T♥-6♣, you have flopped second or middle pair.

Set

Three of a kind. Also called Trips.

Short Stack

A small amount of chips versus the rest of the players at the table. If you have $25 in front of you, and everybody else has over $150, you are on a short stack, or you are short stacked.

Showdown

Showing cards after all community cards have been dealt and all betting is completed.

Side Pot

A separate pot created after any player goes all-in and additional bets are made that exceed the amount of chips the all-in player has. Additional wagers are entered into the side pot, which the all-in player has no chance of winning regardless of his hand.

Slow Play

Representing a strong hand as weak by not betting in order to disguise the strength.

String Bet

Placing a bet then reaching for more chips to raise.

Suited Connector

A hold 'em starting hand in which the two cards are one apart in rank and of the same suit. For example, Q♦-J♦, 3♣-4♣.

Table Stakes

A rule in a poker game meaning that a player may not go into his/her pocket for money during a hand. He/she may only invest the amount of money in front of him/her into the current pot.

Tell

Any personal mannerisms that reveal the quality of one's hand.

Tight

A player who doesn't play many pots. A tight game is one that doesn't have much action.

Tilt

To play wildly or recklessly especially after a bad beat. A player is said to be "on tilt" if he is not playing his best, playing too many hands, trying wild bluffs, raising with bad hands, etc.

Top Pair

A pair with the highest card on the flop. If you have A-Q, and the flop is Q-T-6, you have flopped top pair.

Trips

Three of a kind.

Turn

The fourth community card, put out face-up, by itself. Also known as fourth street.

Under the gun

The first person to have to act when the betting starts before the flop.

Wheel

The lowest hand in lowball and the lowest straight, A-2-3-4-5; also known as a bicycle.

Index